OUR PROMISE TO CHILDREN

OUR PROMISE TO CHILDREN

Edited by:
Kathleen A. Guy

Sponsored by:
The Founders' Network of the Canadian Institute for Advanced Research
&
Centre for Studies of Children at Risk

Published by:
Canadian Institute of Child Health

Preface by:
Fraser Mustard
Head of The Founders' Network
Canadian Institute for Advanced Research

Dan Offord
Director
Centre for Studies of Children at Risk

Karen Goldenberg
President and Chief Operating Officer
Invest in Kids Foundation

Susan E. Young
Treasurer
Imperial Oil Charitable Foundation

Our Promise to Children is being distributed by the Canadian Institute of Child Health (CICH), a national non-profit organization dedicated to improving the overall health and well-being of children in Canada.

To obtain additional copies of *Our Promise to Children*, please contact:

Canadian Institute of Child Health
885 Meadowlands Drive, Suite 512
Ottawa, Ontario
Canada
K2C 3N2

Phone: (613) 224-4144
Fax: (613) 224-4145
E-mail: cich@igs.net
Internet: http://www.cich.ca

ISBN 0-919747-48-5
Printed in Canada

Ce livre est aussi disponible en français sous le titre :
Notre promesse aux enfants
ISBN 0-919747-49-3

This publication does not necessarily represent the views and opinions of Health Canada or the funders or individuals who contributed to the process.

Design, Layout and Production: The HLR Publishing Group, Arnprior, Ontario
Filmwork and Printing: DFR Printing, Pembroke, Ontario
Cover Photo: COMSTOCK

OUR PROMISE TO CHILDREN

PREFACE

An old Ojibway tale tells the story of a time long ago when children of a village became sad and listless, refusing to run or play. The worried adults, after trying everything they could think of, asked Nana'b'oozoo, who was son of a manitou, or spirit, to help their village. Part-manitou, part-man, Nana'b'oozoo was known to love children.

Nana'b'oozoo tried to reawaken the children's vitality and laughter, but instead he scared them. The adults had to ask him to leave the children alone. So he climbed the highest mountain in the land to ask the Creator for advice. The Kitchi-Manitou, or Great Spirit, answered with a riddle: "Even stones have wings." Nana'b'oozoo could not figure out what this meant. In frustration, he threw a handful of coloured pebbles over his shoulder. They turned into lustrous butterflies of every colour, shape and size.

Nana'b'oozoo did not notice this surprising change. He went home thinking he had failed the children, but when they saw the butterflies following him, their eyes lit up. They ran after the tiny, fragile creatures that fluttered in the wind. Since this time, butterflies have been a symbol of children's play and happiness. **1**

This disarmingly simple story tells us some complex truths: that children need to play and laugh, to discover new things. It tells us that children's feelings — their spirits — are important in helping them grow up strong and healthy.

The story also tells us that there is no single saviour for children, no one solution. Nana'b'oozoo does not save the children himself, but the story does not end with his failure. The solution evolves out of the caring and action of those who love children, and comes in many different shapes and forms.

In this story, the mothers and fathers are not left alone to worry over their own children. Instead, the whole village rallies to save its children. Perhaps that is one of the most important aspects of this tale.

Our Promise to Children is about how we in Canada can help all children achieve their potential — and why doing this is essential.

This book is the result of a nationwide collaborative effort involving scores of individuals, including researchers, community workers, child development experts, heads of non-governmental organizations, writers and government officials. It evolved as a direct result of the drafting of national goals in Canada on healthy child and youth development. The document containing eight national goals, *Turning Points*, was released by Health Canada in 1996 (see Appendix D for a list of the goals). *Turning Points* argues that the time has come for change:

"Over the past two decades there have been major advances in knowledge regarding both the factors that influence healthy child development and the negative effects of inadequate social environments on healthy development. These advances in knowledge, coupled with underlying economic and societal changes, call for the development of new strategies designed to improve outcomes for children and youth." **2**

These new strategies should be built on the successes that Canada has already achieved. There has been a lot of progress:

~ dramatic growth in our understanding about human development and what makes people healthy and productive;

~ greater protection for the rights of women and children;

~ better public understanding of social problems such as child abuse, discrimination, crime and poverty; and

~ broader understanding that there can't be a single solution that leads to the well-being of children and families.

This last point is key. The new strategies that *Turning Points* advocates for Canada's children cut across sectors and specialties. The health of the economy and labour market, the ability to compete globally, the strength of communities, the quality of parenting, and the health of social environments all interact. Together, they affect the growth and well-being of children.

Our success as a society will be measured in large part by our ability to bring Canadians together — gathering our talent, our successes, our commitment — around improving the life prospects for all of Canada's children and youth. As we enter the new millennium, what better promise can we make to our children?

BOOK'S SPONSORS

FRASER MUSTARD
The Founders' Network of the Canadian Institute for Advanced Research

DAN OFFORD
Centre for Studies of Children at Risk

KAREN GOLDENBERG
Invest in Kids Foundation

SUSAN E. YOUNG
Imperial Oil Charitable Foundation

ENDNOTES
1. Johnston, 1995
2. Health Canada, 1996, p. 3

ACKNOWLEDGEMENTS

O ur *Promise to Children* is the work of many hands. A full list of the people and organizations who contributed to the book is provided in Appendix F. Their insights, generosity and dedication to helping children are acknowledged with gratitude. Selecting a few of them for special mention risks being unfair to the others, but nevertheless certain outstanding contributions demand recognition.

First of all, the work of the advisory committee was invaluable. The committee was chaired by Dan Offord whose remarkable commitment to children, deep knowledge of the issues, and unfailing support for the project were inspiring. A great debt of gratitude is also due to Fraser Mustard who served as the principal advisor and helped in many other ways. His intellectual leadership and focus on combining knowledge from across disciplines was a driving force in creating this book.

All of the eminent scientists and practitioners on the advisory committee volunteered their time and effort to help inform and refine the content of the book Without their knowledge, and their eagerness to share it, this project would have been impossible.

Jane Bertrand coordinated the research for *Our Promise to Children* and made a major contribution to the text. Her ability, collegial spirit, dedication, and solid professional advice made working with her a pleasure. Cheryl Hamilton worked on the early drafts of many parts of the book. She began the task of pulling together material from many different disciplines and fields into a unified whole. Her skill in this difficult work was extremely important to the project.

Among the funders of this project, Health Canada deserves acknowledgement not only for providing the majority of the financing for *Our Promise to Children*, but also for the knowledgeable support and steady encouragement which its public servants gave to the project from start to finish. The Invest in Kids Foundation, which plays a major role in children's issues, provided both moral and financial support in furtherance of their long-term commitment to raising public awareness. The Imperial Oil Charitable Foundation gave funding as part of the company's impressive focus on Canada's children. Finally, the Department of Justice provided support because of the vision and commitment of its officials to get children off to a good start by strengthening families and as a means of preventing crime.

The collaborative effort of so many people and organizations in producing this book suggests the possibility of an even wider cross-Canada collaboration around helping all children to reach their potential. If this book helps to build that collaboration it will have accomplished its purpose.

INTRODUCTION
Fulfilling Our Potential and Our Promise

"In spite of turbulent times and government restraint, it is not too much to hope that we can make substantial progress in improving the well-being of children and families. Our knowledge of what is possible must be matched by a will to make it a reality. Investing in children is the mark of a compassionate society. It is also enlightened self-interest since today's children are Canada's intellectual, economic and social future." [1]

John Evans, Chairman of Torstar Corporation

"Our children are our future" is an observation frequently intoned by politicians and business and community leaders. Yet — too often — we see public and private sector initiatives that don't consider the interests of children or reach them too late.

If Canada is to survive and thrive as a caring and prosperous society, our leaders — and the rest of us — must do more than pay lip service to the observation that children are the key to our future. We need a much deeper understanding of the importance of the well-being of all Canadian children and undertake the initiatives necessary to promote that well-being. As well, we must abandon the view that, until they reach school age, children are solely the responsibility of their parents. As the research presented in this book makes clear, enormous benefits are to be reaped from programs that support parents in nurturing their children and from community efforts to provide quality care and stimulation for preschoolers.

THE INFORMATION AGE

In the past, Canada has been able to prosper without worrying too much about the strength of its "human capital" — the competence, ingenuity and adaptability of its population. Back then, we could rely on our rich natural resources to drive our economy. But resources are no longer enough in a new economy where information and swift adaptation rule. We now find ourselves in the Information Age, brought on by a shift to a knowledge- and innovation-based economy.

More than anything, today's environment requires people who can think creatively, adapt readily to change, master new technologies, work well with a wide range of people, and continue learning throughout life. Children who don't have a good start in life and in school will find it tougher than ever to complete sufficient education to get a job beyond one in the minimum-wage service sector. Those whose healthy development is weakened by the circumstances in which they grow up will be far less likely to be able to contribute to Canada's economic future.

Giving all children the opportunity to learn, develop their talents and become contributing members of society is both the compassionate and enlightened course to follow — and the key to Canada's future.

NEW LIGHT ON OLD TRUTHS

New research from neuroscience, along with the results of long-term social science studies, shed new light on old truths and help us understand why certain factors in the lives of children and their families have the effects they do.

Our Promise to Children relies on published data, research and analysis by experts in fields related to child development, mainly from Canada but also from other countries. It relies, too, on the experience of people involved in community initiatives aimed at improving the lives of children.

Some of the research is confirming what caring parents have known all along. For example, most people instinctively know that young children need to be hugged and played with, but now neuroscientists are providing the biological basis for the benefits of early physical nurturing. Recent research results reveal that parents and other caregivers who smile, soothe, talk and play with young children are, in the process, actually helping the infant brain organize itself into patterns that will assist the child's learning and coping in later life. Through their natural expression of physical affection, these adults are providing the experiences, or inputs, that the developing brain needs.

As our understanding of what influences child development expands, we are finding that what happens in the first few years of a child's life has major, long-lasting effects on the capacity of the child — and later the adult — to learn and to adjust to life's ups and downs. Good early care-giving that stimulates learning and loving, along with positive supports and experiences during childhood and adolescence, can significantly affect the pathways of development.

While neurosciences are telling us about brain development, social sciences research that began decades ago to track the history of children in families is yielding some compelling findings. These studies are providing information about what helps or hinders children and young people to mature into healthy, well-adjusted adults.

The research on child development by both biological and social scientists which is highlighted in *Our Promise to Children* points toward the following themes:

— **Early is crucial.** What happens in the first few years of life can have a lifelong impact on health, mental ability and coping skills.

— **Getting a good start is key, but it is not enough.** There is no such thing as a one-shot inoculation for healthy development. Care and sup-port are needed all along the developmental path into adulthood.

— **Environments and experiences are as important as, or even more important than, genetic make-up in affecting later health and com-petence.** All the places where children live, learn, grow and play affect their development. Families come first, but families thrive or flounder within a wider context that includes neighbourhoods, workplaces, voluntary organiza-tions, schools, communities and government.

— **A second chance can get a young life back on track.** Children who begin life in difficult circumstances can bounce back later if they get what they missed early in life — it's just more difficult and expensive. Human beings have enormous potential to overcome adversity.

— **Relationships are critical; one caring and competent adult in a child's life can make a tremendous difference.** Social supports — relation-ships with loved ones, friends and colleagues — are widely believed to influence the health of adults. The same is true, only more so, for young people growing up. Just one significant adult can make a world of difference in a child's life.

THE DETERMINANTS OF OPTIMAL CHILD DEVELOPMENT

Researchers are beginning to understand what it takes for a child to grow up healthy and happy. Those needs are called the determinants of healthy development. It's not a perfect science. Sometimes a child who seems to have everything just right grows up wrong. And there are cases when children seem to overcome all odds. Despite a horrific childhood, some people still thrive and become accomplished adults.

Our Promise to Children is organized around what children need from their social environment to develop fully. These needs of children — or determinants of optimal child development — are grouped under four main categories:

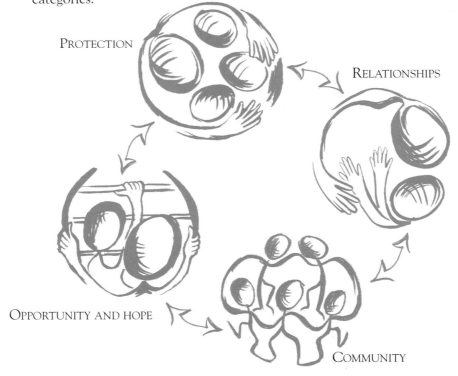

PROTECTION

RELATIONSHIPS

OPPORTUNITY AND HOPE

COMMUNITY

Not all children, however, live in the kind of Canada where these four basic needs or determinants are met. Not all families are caring or have a decent income. And not all communities have the resources to give them a helping hand. The result is that too many children in Canada are never given the chance to live life to its fullest. Some die needlessly, others get sick or are injured due to neglect. Many more end up trapped in a childhood of poverty. The adults in prisons and detox centres were all once babies, filled with potential.

HOW ARE CANADA'S CHILDREN FARING?

The Canadian Council on Social Development seeks to measure Canada's progress in providing opportunities for children to grow and develop to their potential. The Council's 1996 report, *The Progress of Canada's Children*, found some encouraging signs. **2** Infant mortality has fallen steadily over the last 30 years, death by injury has dropped for children under the age of 19, youth literacy is high, and Canada has one of the world's highest rates of enrolment in university and other post-secondary schools.

The report also found that there is no room for Canadians to be smug. Teen suicide has increased dramatically over the last 30 years and is now the second leading cause of death among teenagers: 13 deaths for every 100,000 teens. Families are finding it hard to balance their responsibilities at home with the demands of work. Parents are being forced to work longer hours to cope with falling incomes. And many children are living in families where their parents have been unemployed or fear losing their jobs.

As well, health remains a concern despite the benefits of the Canadian health care system. Almost six percent of all babies were born with a low birth weight in 1994, which can leave them more susceptible to ill health.

The report also expressed other concerns:

~ Roughly one out of every five children under the age of 18 lives in poverty, based on Statistics Canada's measure of low income.

~ Cuts to funding for kindergarten programs have occurred right across Canada.

~ Too many children are experimenting with tobacco and alcohol at an early age, increasing the odds they'll be hooked. For example, one in six children in Canada has tried smoking by age 11.

~ Violent crimes by youth 12 to 17 years of age doubled between 1986 and 1992.

~ The cost of raising a child is high — an estimated $150,000 from birth to age 18 (this sum excludes the cost of university).

Do you want to know more about how Canada's children are doing? Look up Appendix A, "Canada's Kids: Thriving or Just Surviving?" for more information. Based on data provided by the Canadian Council on Social Development **E1** and the federal government's National Longitudinal Survey on Children and Youth (NLSCY), **E2** this appendix is the work of the Vanier Institute of the Family. New and updated data will be available shortly.

To find out where to get updated statistics on the state of Canada's children, and how to get information from organizations that are gathering and analysing data related to children, youth and families, refer also to Appendix C.

CHILDREN HAVE RIGHTS

The nations of the world have set out the entitlements of children in the United Nations Convention on the Rights of the Child. This Convention was signed and ratified by Canada, in recognition of the shared responsibility of all Canadians for the well-being of our nation's children. It recognizes such rights as the right to survival, the right to protection and the right to develop.

What all this means is that we, as a society, have a responsibility to children.

The responsibility of society does not take away from the responsibility of parents to raise their children as best they can. As the Convention says, the family is the fundamental group in society and it should be afforded the necessary protection and assistance so that it can fully assume its responsibilities within the community.

But families do not exist in a vacuum. Parents bring home the stresses or successes of the workplace and daily life. Their income helps determine the kind of circumstances in which their children live. Children come into contact with all sorts of people as they grow up — neighbours, child care providers, friends, teachers and other members of the community. Children's social environment — poverty or prosperity, opportunity or discrimination, violence or tranquility — affects them profoundly.

KEEPING OUR PROMISES

Every human being is born with a set of strengths and weaknesses: every person has potential. What happens to that potential depends largely on experience. Childhood is the most vulnerable period of human development, and by far the most influential. If the experiences of children support healthy development, they will be more likely to fulfil their potential as adults.

Children do not start out life on an equal footing and every child is different. But all children deserve an equal chance to achieve their life dreams. If they don't get that chance, Canada as a nation will not live up to its potential either.

Our children depend on us. It is within our grasp to put into practice what we know will make a difference for them. As parents, relatives, neighbours and members of society, we share this responsibility. *Our Promise to Children* is about specific things we can do to help our children achieve their potential.

CHILDREN'S VOICES: "KEEP YOUR PROMISES" E3

In 1993, Health Canada interviewed children and teenagers for a video called Kids Talk and Videotape. The places in which these children and teenagers lived were quite different — from inner city apartment complexes to small communities in rural Canada. Many of the concerns, however, were the same: parents who didn't get along or who had split up, parents who worried all the time about paying the bills, the struggle of young people to be understood, the threat of drugs and alcohol and AIDS ... the future.

Children's wishes were among the most poignant. They said, "I wish I'd see my mom a lot more." – "I'd have a dad because I don't." — "No drugs, no nothing, like perfect, a nice big house and a nice yard and stuff." — "I'd wish the violence would stop. There's so much violence in this world."

The children's worries spoke volumes, too. Their concerns ranged from the very personal to the apocalyptic. "I want to be successful to show my father he was wrong." — "Ease up on us. I think a lot of adults expect us to be perfect when we can't be." — "I'm afraid of the future. I don't want to be walking around wearing a gas mask."

Some of them had seen a lot already. "What makes me sad is I see some of the families are really poor and the parents are alcoholics and the kids don't get attention." — "The only good neighbourhoods are the rich neighbourhoods, and how many kids grow up there?"

They were very clear about what families are for: love and security. "I love my family and it's a good thing in life to have." They wanted adults to listen and care. "Treat us the way you'd want to be treated." — "Keep your promises."

ENDNOTES
1. Evans, 1996, p.14-15
2. Canadian Council on Social Development, 1996

EXHIBIT ENDNOTES
E1. Canadian Council on Social Development, 1996
E2. Human Resources Development Canada & Statistics Canada, 1996
E3. Health Canada, 1993. Quotations from *Kids Talk and Videotape*

Section I
How Do Children Develop?

Chapter 1
THE MIND MATTERS:
A Child's Developing Brain

Many things we need can wait, the child cannot.
Now is the time his bones are being formed,
his blood is being made,
his mind is being developed.
To him we cannot say tomorrow,
his name is today.

Gabriela Mistral, Chilean poet

A CHILD'S DEVELOPING MIND: EARLY STIMULATION IS KEY

When people think about children growing up, images of external change come to mind. Children get taller year by year and start to "fill out." Children pass milestones of learning to walk and talk and tie their shoes. But inside, there's another kind of growing going on. The brain is also developing. The new knowledge from the science of neurobiology is expanding our understanding of this internal process.

We now have clear, scientific evidence of how stimulation in the early years affects the development of emotions, thinking and behaviour. Brain development in the early years of life is critical. It has tremendous impact on the ability of children to reach their full potential in life.

A WORK IN PROGRESS ❶

A lot of brain development occurs in the womb. A full-term baby comes into the world with a nervous system made up of 100 billion nerve cells, called neurons. But the brain has far from finished its development. The newborn's neurons are not yet connected into the intricate patterns that characterize the mature human brain.

These neurons must develop in different ways early in life to perform their different functions. Together, they form a complex network of connections that are essential for an individual to think, feel or move. The connections among neurons allow the neurons to communicate with each other and to control the body's organs, glands and muscles.

From the day of birth, a baby's brain must begin sorting itself out and preparing for a complex world. Much of this happens in the first 12 months of life, but the process does continue for the next decade or so.

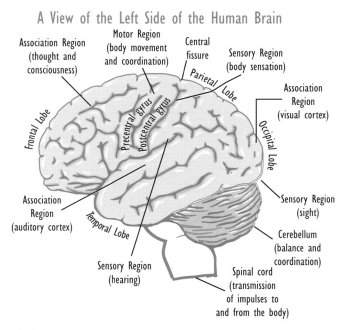

A View of the Left Side of the Human Brain

Association Region (thought and consciousness)

Motor Region (body movement and coordination)

Central fissure

Sensory Region (body sensation)

Parietal Lobe

Association Region (visual cortex)

Frontal Lobe

Precentral gyrus

Postcentral gyrus

Occipital Lobe

Association Region (auditory cortex)

Temporal Lobe

Sensory Region (sight)

Cerebellum (balance and coordination)

Sensory Region (hearing)

Spinal cord (transmission of impulses to and from the body)

The human brain is an amazing and complex organ that allows each of us to think, feel and act. In turn, the brain systems that allow us to think, feel and act are shaped by experience.

At birth, the brain has established only the initial connections and paths among its billions of neurons. A newborn's brain has all the brain areas and neurons, but only a portion of the brain is "wired" and ready to go. After birth, there's a frenzy of activity in which the neurons connect with each other to form the neural networks that enable movement, talking, feeling and thinking. This process is driven in large part not by heredity, but by the flood of sensory stimulation that a child receives from the outside world.

The stimulation (sights, sounds, touches, smells and tastes) the brain receives during these critical or sensitive periods drives the formation of the connections between the neurons. The electrical activity of brain cells, triggered by sensory stimulation, changes the physical structure of the brain. Neurons that are not used are discarded.

The critical period for the development of core functions, such as arousal, behaviour and emotion, occurs during the first few years of life. Adults' interactions with the child during this sensitive early period provide the stimulation that will influence how the child's brain develops and how he or she responds to new situations and challenges.

If a baby is cared for by an adult who is intensely involved with the child, the baby and the adult normally establish what we call an attachment relationship (refer to Chapter 7 for a more detailed discussion on attachment). Attachment provides safety and security to the infant and growing young child and establishes wiring patterns in the brain which can reduce anxiety and allow the brain to better take in and incorporate new sensory stimulation.

Most parents want to hold and cuddle their children, talk to them, and give them toys and other playthings. This kind of stimulation does more than make children smile. It strengthens their capacity to learn and to cope emotionally with life's stresses. Providing care and stimulation in the early years of a child's development offers huge rewards in developmental terms.

On the other hand, neglecting or abusing an infant during this critical period can produce functions and wiring patterns in the core of the brain that can lead to heightened anxiety in response to stimuli and to abnormal and negative behaviour in childhood and adult life. Children who are abused (physically or sexually) early in life, or are in abusive family environments, are at risk in the development of core brain functions that are exquisitely sensitive to what the child experiences. [2]

It has long been known that neglect and abuse can impair child development. Neuroscientists are now investigating how these assaults on a child's development may affect the biological reaction to stressful events. The seeds of adult aggression and lack of emotional control may be sown in the brain wiring of some children who receive very little care and nurturing in their early years.

The brain's great spurt of development draws to a close around the age of 10. By this time, the brain will have destroyed the weakest connections, preserving only those that have been well established by experience. While the value of stimulation in early childhood has been recognized for some time, it is only now that this can be quantified and explained through evidence from neuroscience. Quite simply, we now know that early experience shapes our biology.

According to Clyde Hertzman, with the Department of Health Care and Epidemiology at the University of British Columbia in Vancouver, "the period from pre-conception to age 5 can be referred to as the investment phase for child development. Research now demonstrates that this period is much more important than we ever realized before. Studies in neurobiology, neurodevelopment and early intervention show that conception to age 5 is an extremely sensitive and critically important time in mental and emotional development. During this investment phase, children develop language skills, the ability to learn, to cope with stress, to have healthy relationships with others, and to have a sense of self. Health, well-being and competence also have roots in the earliest experiences in life and, through the parents, in the period before conception. Failure to provide optimum conditions for a child's development during this time makes the developing brain physically different from the brain of children who have been well nurtured, and these differences can have lifelong consequences." [3]

NEUROSCIENCE AND CHILDREN: SOME OBSERVATIONS [E1]

▲ Brain development before age 1 is more rapid and extensive than previously realized.

▲ Brain development is more vulnerable to environmental influences than suspected.

▲ The effects of early environment are long lasting.

▲ The environment affects the number of brain cells and the way they are "wired."

▲ We now have evidence of the negative impact of early stress on brain development and function.

This book only introduces the story of brain development, competence and coping skills. It is part of the context for discussing the determinants of optimal child development. Readers who are interested in understanding more fully the new research in developmental neurobiology or new research in the area of early childhood development (discussed in upcoming chapters) may want to turn to the following sources:

~ "How a Child's Brain Develops" in *Time*, June 9, 1997;

~ "Your Child: From Birth to Three" in *Newsweek* Special Edition, Spring/Summer 1997;

~ *Starting Points* (1994), Carnegie Corporation of New York;

~ *Rethinking the Brain: New Insights into Early Development* (1997), Rima Shore, Families and Work Institute, New York;

~ *Developing Minds: Challenge and Continuity Across the Life Span* (1993), Michael & Margorie Rutter, Penguin Books, London, Eng.;

~ *Galen's Prophecy* (1994), Jerome Kagan, HarperCollins Publishers, Inc, New York;

~ *The Moral Intelligence of Children* (1997) Robert Coles; and

~ *Overcoming the Odds: High Risk Children from Birth to Adulthood* (1992), Emmy Werner & Ruth Smith, Cornell University Press, Ithaca, New York.

Neuroscience is complex, but the bottom line is simple — early stimulation and nurturing are critical to later brain functioning, competence and the ability to cope with stress.

SEEDS OF AGGRESSION E2

Like humans, rhesus monkeys live in social groups and exhibit complex interpersonal and group relationships. Infant monkeys spend their first six months close to their mothers, gradually spending increasing amounts of time playing with other monkeys in the social group.

In laboratory experiments, infant monkeys were separated from their mothers and peers for those first six months. In other words, these monkeys were deprived of the comfort and security of normal nurturing. They developed severe behavioural problems, including withdrawal and aggression.

Reintroduced into a group, they tended to be fearful or start fights with other monkeys their own age. Some were able to adopt some social skills and get along in a group but as soon as a stressful event occurred — such as the arrival of a newcomer — these monkeys reverted to old behaviours. They were also unable to perform complex tasks as well as other monkeys. The female monkeys raised in isolation were not interested in mating; if they had young, they were unable to nurture them.

In other studies, monkeys raised for the first six months with peers, but without the care of a mother or other adult, were aggressive toward strangers in adolescence, and were more likely to be expelled from their social group than their mother-reared counterparts.

In addition to the behavioural changes that were observed, scientists have also recently identified changes in brain chemistry that may occur in response to acute stress. The aggressive, maladjusted monkeys raised without a nurturing adult were found to have unusually low levels of a brain chemical called serotonin.

Studies have suggested that serotonin acts to reduce aggressive behaviour, and another brain chemical, vasopressin, acts to increase it. Drugs to stimulate

ENDNOTES
1. Hertzman & Mustard, 1997; Cyander & Mustard, 1997. The following discussion on brain development during the early years is based on these two articles from *Entropy*, Spring 1997, Vol. 1 Issue 1.
2. Perry, 1995
3. Hertzman, interview

serotonin levels have been used to treat uncontrollable aggressive behaviour in children. Investigations are under way to learn more about the interaction of these two brain chemicals.

Animal studies permit researchers to: **E3**
▲ control many factors such as genetic make-up, diet, early experiences and other aspects of the social and physical environment;
▲ conduct research on the effects of various types of treatments which would be impossible to conduct with humans; and
▲ track the complete life cycle of many animals over a relatively short period of time.
There is a 95 percent or higher overlap of the genetic code between humans and non-human primates, such as rhesus monkeys.

The early period after birth may not be the only period in which the young are particularly vulnerable to developmental problems caused by maltreatment. Golden hamsters, which go through a clearly defined adolescent period similar to puberty in humans, were given the equivalent of a troubled adolescence in one experiment. Each was put into a cage with an older, larger hamster who nipped, chased and generally abused the smaller one.

It was found that these young hamsters in turn picked on smaller hamsters to an abnormal degree and were unusually fearful of other animals their own size. They exhibited what researchers termed "a volatile mixture of fearfulness, hypervigilance and the misinterpretation of threats — a recipe for violence." **E4** In a related study, the same behaviours were induced by adding a stress hormone directly into the brains of some hamsters.

There is still much we do not understand about the impact of abuse and the origins of aggressive behaviour, but animal studies such as these allow researchers to look closely at the neurological and biological effects of early stress and trauma on human development.

EXHIBIT ENDNOTES
E1. Mustard 1996 in Keating & Mustard, 1996
E2. Ferris, 1996
E3. Myers, 1996; Keating, 1992
E4. Ferris, 1996, p. 26

Chapter 2
NO TIME TO WASTE:
Early Experiences Are Key

There is much we still do not understand about human development. In general, we cannot provide an exact answer to the question "What made that child turn into this adult?" But new research has revealed some fascinating clues about what goes on in the growth process of a human being.

As highlighted in the previous chapter, new information is coming from our ability, using the latest technology, to examine cells and molecules. Scientists are finding out more about the chemicals in the brain that activate certain responses, and about the interactions between the central nervous system (the brain and spinal cord) and other systems of the body, such as the immune system.

There is mounting evidence — not only from neuroscience but also developmental psychology, social sciences and education — that what happens in the first few years of life can have major, long-lasting effects on the capacity of the person to be healthy, to learn and to cope with life's challenges.

Two powerful forces are at work in the development of a child. Both interact with one another and influence the growth and well-being of a child right through to adulthood:

▲ nature, or the genetic programming that a child brings into the world; and

▲ nurture, or the experiences each child has during life.

INTERPLAY OF NATURE AND NURTURE

Our new understanding of the impact of early experiences puts the nature/nurture debate into a different perspective. We now know why nurturing has a substantial effect on behaviour, IQ, competence and coping skills.

Harvard's Jerome Kagan writes in his book, *Galen's Prophecy*: "The power of genes is real but limited — a principle that operates even during the growth of the embryo .... If a mother drinks too much alcohol during her pregnancy, the brain of the newborn can be very different from that of most infants. No human quality, physical or psychological, is free of the contribution of events within and outside the organism. Development is a cooperative mission." ❶

An example of this interplay of nature and nurture is the development of language. The ability to learn language is strongest in early childhood. Most children learn to talk, using single words and simple phrases, when they are around 1 year to 18 months old. Every child is genetically programmed to learn to talk, but the language depends on what they hear. They learn by listening and by trying to speak.

The language that a child responds to, and which activates the brain, is language that is part of the dynamic of human caring and interaction. Background noise, like that from a television or radio, does not have much impact on brain development. However, playing peek-a-boo while cuddling and making eye contact with a child, for example, does.

During babies' babbling phase at around 6 months, they make all the sounds used by all languages spoken by humans around the world. Eventually, however, the baby's ability to make these sounds diminishes. The language a baby hears stimulates particular neurons in the brain's cortex to connect with each other. These pathways become well used and the baby develops the power to understand and use language. At the same time, other neurons, stimulated by sounds not in the language which surrounds a baby, are not used and no connections are made. Hence, the baby's diminishing ability to make certain sounds.

The brain development of a baby who does not get a lot of verbal stimulation is negatively affected. Pictures of the brain's cortex show us how dramatic the impact can be: there is actually less activity and fewer connections in the brain. Not surprisingly, the child has less ability to communicate.

LONG-LASTING EFFECTS OF EARLY EXPERIENCES

"Early experiences can improve intellectual flexibility. They can help make children physically strong and emotionally resilient, or they can contribute to a negative spiral of risk and vulnerability," observes Daniel Keating, chair of the Human Development Program of the Canadian Institute for Advanced Research. [2]

Children who have an adverse early childhood can have difficulty in coping with the school system when they enter kindergarten because of difficulties in thinking and behaviour. Boys who cannot cope show disruptive behaviour at this stage and tend to do poorly in school. As many as 25 percent of the boys identified as disruptive when they enter kindergarten report delinquent behaviours by the age of 14. [3]

Studies in Canada and the United States have revealed a sudden decline in intellectual functioning, starting around the age of 18 to 24 months and continuing through the preschool period, among children from families with very low socioeconomic status. Socioeconomic status is measured in terms of factors such as parental income and level of education. These children didn't start life with lower intellectual potential. Gillian Doherty-Derkowski, author of *Quality Matters: Excellence in Early Childhood Programs*, writes "the decline in intellectual functioning starting around 18 months is believed to result from a lack of language stimulation and opportunities to play with a variety of materials during the toddler and preschool years." [4]

It's important to note that children from low-income groups are not the only ones who are developmentally vulnerable if there is inadequate stimulation in the toddler and preschool years. Middle-class children who were enrolled in low-quality preschools and other early education programs demonstrated lower language and intellectual skills than children who were in programs that provided a safe and stimulating environment in which to play and learn. Several studies have shown that children who spent time in settings where caregivers were consistently unresponsive, and where there were few planned activities, tended to engage in aimless wandering. Their language development was delayed and they tended to interact poorly with other children. [5]

Although supportive interventions in the school period can turn some of these problems around, the effect is limited. On the other hand, there is now considerable evidence from social science research that early interventions that enhance the quality of stimulation for children in difficult circumstances can have a very positive effect. They substantially reduce the behavioural problems when the children enter the school system and enhance their learning capacity, coping skills and competence.

Studies of both animals and humans dramatically illustrate the strong and long-lasting impact of early interventions. Here are some examples.

Perry Preschool Project: ❻ In a now-well-known experiment during the 1960s, children who took part in a preschool program between ages 3 and 6 were doing much better by the age of 27 than the control group who did not attend the preschool program.

The Perry Preschool Project was an early childhood compensatory educational program for 3- and 4-year-olds who were at high risk. The program offered a special curriculum for the children and also educated and supported their parents, particularly mothers. At 27 years, those who took part in the program as children had completed more schooling, had fewer criminal problems, less drug use, were more likely to be employed, were less likely to be on social assistance, and had fewer mental health problems than those who had not taken part.

It's estimated that for every dollar spent in this compensatory program, $7 were saved over the next 20 years.

Right Start: ❼ A group of preschool children from a low-income neighbourhood with many problems participated in a kindergarten program to help them learn basic number concepts. At the end of the program these children showed a better understanding of numbers than children in a control group from the same neighbourhood who did not participate in the mathematics program. The effects did not stop there. In later school years, the children from the low-income neighbourhood who had participated in the kindergarten mathematics program did better than a control group of children from a middle-class background.

The Carolina Abecedarian Project: ❽ This experiment began in the 1970s to find out if educational enrichment at a very early age could prevent declines in mental development that often accompany extreme poverty. Between 3 weeks and 3 months of age, infants in the experimental group were enrolled in a quality child care program which lasted until they entered kindergarten. Children in both the control and experimental groups received nutrition and health services, so the primary difference was the quality child care program. Intelligence test scores were gathered on the children regularly and, from infancy on into their school years, there were clear differences. The children who attended the child care program had higher scores — their thinking abilities (particularly reading, writing and general knowledge) were clearly enhanced by the early child care experience.

Stephen Suomi's (a primatologist in Maryland) rhesus monkeys: [9] A group of monkeys which were treated badly in their early years show various problems dealing with challenges. The males tend to be withdrawn, and are often forced to leave the troop or be killed by other group members. The females that were treated badly when they were young, in turn, are unable to nurture their offspring. They also have difficulty with challenges and stress. But if a non-biological but competent "mother" is placed in the same physical space with the biological mother and child, the child monkey does well. The young monkey will develop the competence and coping skills to get along with the troop, and rear and nurture their young.

Rats, early nurturing and stress: [10] Just as stress in early childhood can hinder brain development, effective nurturing may improve the future adult's ability to handle life's stresses.

An experiment on rats at McGill University in Montreal, although it cannot provide firm conclusions about human babies, suggests some important possibilities. In the experiment, newborn rats that were gently handled for 15 minutes a day for 21 days were found to have undergone a permanent physical change in their brains. The density of the receptor cells for stress hormones increased. These receptor cells — in both rat brains and human brains — alert the brain that there are stress hormones in the bloodstream; the brain then regulates the numbers, reducing the amount of stress hormone produced. Because they had more receptors, the baby rats produced lower quantities of stress hormones and were better able to control stress reactions.

The non-threatening stimulation rats received in their first three weeks — which are equivalent to approximately two years of a human life-span — appears to have benefited them throughout life. They learned better and faster than their non-handled peers and they were healthier over their lifetimes. Rats that received the same nurturing treatment later in life did not show the same benefits. Early intervention was the key.

FOR A LIFETIME...

In the early years, there are sensitive or critical periods when children need nurturing and stimulation to help them develop. High-quality early childhood education services, including affordable child care and support for parents in all sectors of the society, are crucial for the children and for the future of society. The 7000 babies born in Canada this week are beginning the process of wiring their brains for a lifetime. This process will have a large influence on their behaviour and capacity to learn throughout the rest of their lives. There is no time to waste — their early experiences will make a big difference to all of us.

The next chapter discusses how children who begin life in difficult circumstances can bounce back later if they get what they missed early in life.

ENDNOTES
1. Kagan, 1994, p. 37
2. Keating, 1996. Presentation at the Symposium on National Projects for a New Canada. March 2, 1996
3. Tremblay et al, 1994
4. Doherty-Derkowski, 1995, p. 9
5. Rubenstein & Howes, 1979; Howes et al, 1988, in Doherty-Derkowski, 1995
6. Schweinhart et al, 1993
7. Case, 1997
8. Campbell & Ramey, 1994
9. Suomi, 1991, 1988; Suomi, 1993
10. Meaney et al, 1988, reported in Ferris, 1996

Chapter 3
BOUNCING BACK:
Children's Resilience

Children need to get off to a good start in life. That begins even before birth with mothers eating right and avoiding tobacco, alcohol and drugs. And, as we have seen, the first few years after birth are a critical foundation for life.

That's not to say that resources should be directed only at young children. Older children and teens continue to need help along the way to reach their full potential. Communities have to be supportive of their children right from the start and the support has to continue all the way through the teen years. But it's far more successful and cost-effective to prevent problems along the way than to cure them later. It's far cheaper to ensure that pregnant women get a proper diet than to deal with low birth weight babies who may end up needing a lifetime of support. It's far better for society to get children off to a good start when they enter school than to provide programs that help teen dropouts get back into the education system.

A critical question is: when is it too late to repair the damage caused by abuse or neglect? Research shows that children who begin life in difficult circumstances can bounce back later if they get what they missed early in life — it's just more difficult and expensive.

RESILIENCE AND RISK

Some children start out with the odds stacked against them. But no child can be guaranteed a life free from stress and problems — no matter how hard parents try. Everyone learns sooner or later about loss, rejection, pressure and failure. Whatever comes along, children need to be able to cope, surmount difficulty, get over disappointment and try again.

Effectively managing both life's opportunities and challenges requires the qualities of resilience and perseverance. Our task is to find the best ways of instilling these qualities in all children.

Paul Steinhauer, a child psychiatrist at The Hospital for Sick Children in Toronto, focuses much of his work on helping children from disadvantaged backgrounds. He defines resilience as "very good adaptation to severe stress, and/or the ability to rebound to prestress levels of adaptation." ❶ Children whose lives are full of negative experiences or influences are less likely to develop the flexibility and confidence that lead to resilience.

Risks have a multiplier effect when they cluster. Just as people who are worn out and under stress are more likely to get sick, children whose lives are overloaded with risks are more likely to have difficulties. A British study concluded that four risk factors interacting with one another could multiply the likelihood of distress tenfold. ❷ For example, being the child of a single mother does not, in and of itself, make a child more vulnerable. But if a single mother is poor, lives in substandard housing in a tough neighbourhood and is isolated and depressed, her child is more likely to suffer ill health and other problems than children in less risky circumstances.

The more risks there are in a child's life, the more important it is to create buffers against those risks. A child who has been neglected will need more people around to show they care, and more opportunities to build relationships of trust and friendship, than a child who has learned from birth that adults provide comfort and love.

"JUST A LITTLE BIT OF QUALITY TOWARD ME"

A study based on the experiences of 19 Canadian young people identified as "successful" graduates of the Ontario child welfare system points to some key factors in overcoming early childhood deprivation. Seven men and 12 women between the ages of 16 and 26 were asked to talk about what experiences helped them gain confidence and well-being, despite their difficult early years. The study was conducted by Susan Silva-Wayne of the Faculty of Social Work, Wilfrid Laurier University, in Waterloo, Ontario. ❸

These young people had been through an average of nine years in out-of-home care, either in a foster family or in group care. Each had had an average of three different foster or group homes. One woman had been with a foster family for 22 years. One of the young men had been through about eight placements, half of them neglectful or abusive. The reasons for being placed in out-of-home care included physical, emotional and sexual abuse; parental mental illness, alcoholism or death in the family; chronic neglect; abandonment; relinquishment shortly after birth; and chronic spousal abuse.

The criteria for identifying successful graduates from the child welfare system were based on the development of individual potential, not just on formal educational or financial status. Most members of the group, however, were attending university or college at the time of the study. The few who had not continued past high school planned to pursue educational goals in the future.

All of these young people felt doubly devalued. First, they had come from problem homes. Secondly, they faced the stigma of being raised in foster care or group homes. To overcome this double problem, they had to learn to protect themselves, to be assertive and self-reliant and to challenge the low expectations of other people.

The one factor that seemed to make the most difference in the lives of these young people was having caring people in their lives — a role model, a member of a supportive community, an adult who reinforced a positive self-image, someone who gave them an opportunity. Individuals such as these help open up new pathways, by providing a series of new opportunities that can help change a young person's life course. Silva-Wayne gives some illustrations of her findings:

~ "Pathfinders" helped the youngsters navigate through systems. For example, a neighbour helped a new immigrant choose high school courses that would make her eligible for university.

~ One young man who dreamt of becoming a police officer was inspired by an officer who came to school to teach about bicycle safety.

Silva-Wayne also cites the positive role that community can play in the lives of these youngsters by providing consistent new opportunities, as distinct from one-time interventions. "Community" covers a wide spectrum of supportive environments at school, in recreational opportunities and in numerous other settings. The children's self-esteem was built mainly through interactions with others, including family members, professional helpers, foster-family members, volunteers, friends and teachers who recognized and respected the young people's goals and contributed to their achievement.

~ One mother made sure her child was tested by the education system before the family split apart; the child was placed in a gifted class which provided a source of adult support and peer friendships.

~ Some were fortunate to find support for their emerging identities in their foster or group home.

~ Others were sustained by ethnic or cultural groups or by religious communities that enhanced their sense of identity. One young Aboriginal man had turned to the elders in his community for education and healing.

~ One young person recalled a teacher who gave "just a little bit of quality toward me. It was so small and so tiny it was almost invisible. I guess a child from a functional-type home wouldn't even realize that had an effect on your life at all ... To me though, it was incredible, just because it was something I didn't usually get." **4**

Gaining opportunities was a critical factor in the success of these disadvantaged youngsters. A support centre that helped prepare young people for independence from the child welfare system helped some to acquire employment skills, find work, get information on education and housing, and build friendships with other young people who knew what it was like to be in care. Sometimes opportunities came from the education system. On the other hand, some of these young people expressed frustration with what they felt were additional obstacles for disadvantaged children: race, gender and class bias.

This was a small anecdotal study, but it conveys a sense of how people can overcome adversity and build new lives, given a chance, and how "just a little bit of quality" from an adult can make an immense difference to a young person.

OVERCOMING THE ODDS

Emmy Werner is Professor of Human Development and Research Child Psychologist at the University of California, Davis. Werner and colleagues began a study of 698 children born in 1955 in a community on Kauai, one of the Hawaiian islands. **5**

About one third of the children in this study faced obstacles to healthy development, including a difficult birth (which can cause physical or mental disabilities), chronic poverty and family problems like mental illness or alcoholism. Two out of three of these children at risk had developed serious behavioural or learning problems by age 10, been in trouble with the law, experienced mental health problems, or been pregnant before they were 18 years old.

Werner set out to discover what had happened to those who had avoided these problems and grown up to become competent and caring adults, and whether the problems experienced by the others were the beginning of a series of troubles and failures.

The advantage of Werner's study is that she has tracked her subjects over decades, into their forties. Her findings led her to an important conclusion: it is possible to recover, throughout a lifetime, from early difficulties and degradations. "Early life is important for laying the foundation for competence, good health and trust, but there are major opportunities for changes later on." **6**

If you look at troubled teens over time, she says you'll see that many of them do find their way back on track. Most delinquent teens do not become hardened criminals; many who drop out of school eventually go back; most teenaged moms are off public assistance and working by the time their own children are in school.

What contributed most to the well-being of these young people and their successful transition to adulthood? The key factor was having at least one person who accepted them for themselves, who rewarded them for helpfulness and cooperation, who gave them some challenges, who encouraged their interests, who contributed to their self-esteem, or who provided a model for living. Many of the children who overcame the odds had a close family member who provided unconditional acceptance and created trust in early life. A neighbour, a caring teacher or an elder in the community helped some of these children by supporting them and teaching them skills. Some of those who had difficulty early on found a sustaining relationship later in life with a spouse or a mentor who had faith in them.

Later opportunities that also made a positive difference were membership in a church or other faith community, joining the Armed Forces (which provided a sense of belonging, stability and career prospects), further education after high school, being able to do some form of public service, and a job or career position, especially if a mentor was there to provide counselling and advice.

These findings transcend ethnic, social class, geographical and historical boundaries, says Werner. "One of the most important things that has come out of our study and others is a sense of hope." [6]

Werner's study and others illustrate some of the factors that contribute to resilience, in spite of the odds stacked against children. But the answer is not only to look for ways to build in resilience or to fortify children's capacity to cope in order to survive even more risks. Childhood poverty, for example, can have a negative impact on lifelong development. In the short run, helping to build resilience of children living in poverty can make a big difference. However, the preferred long-term strategy is not to build resilience into poor children, but to eliminate child poverty. We have a collective responsibility to create the kinds of social and physical environments that enable children to thrive.

The next chapter discusses how our country's economic future depends largely on what happens to our children today, and why investing in high quality social and physical environments makes good economic sense.

ENDNOTES

1. Steinhauer, interview
2. Rutter, 1979 in Silva-Wayne, 1995
3. Silva-Wayne, 1995
4. Silva-Wayne, 1995, p. 317
5. Werner & Smith, 1992
6. Werner, 1996: Presentation June 13 to a public forum of the Centre for Studies of Children at Risk, Hamilton, Ontario

Chapter 4
MORE REASONS TO INVEST IN CHILDREN:
Child Development and a Changing World

INVESTING IN CHILDREN IS VITAL TO OUR ECONOMY

"During this period of rapid change, it is important to recognize the interdependence of economic and social development. Successful 'new economies' will place a high premium on knowledge and innovation, which depend on a society's human resources. Failure to invest in all stages of human development, particularly the early years, will negatively affect future economic prosperity in two ways. First, we may lack the human resources needed to sustain future economic growth. Second, we may increase the social burden arising from problems that begin early in an individual's development and that then create multiple costs for the individual and for society over time." ❶

Daniel Keating and Fraser Mustard

OUR ECONOMIC FUTURE IS AT STAKE

Children are seldom viewed as part of the economy. But the well-being of children has a direct impact on the future economic health of Canada. It is vital to recognize that today's children are tomorrow's workforce. That is increasingly important as society places ever greater requirements for education, training, innovation and flexibility on its workers. In fact, there are two major economic issues swirling around Canadian children at the end of the twentieth century.

The first is the Information Revolution that is sweeping the world. A whole new economic structure is emerging, based on computers and telecommunications, that is changing the way people live and work. Because this revolution is based on brains, not brawn, it is more important than ever to develop a workforce that has strong cognitive abilities, and the coping skills required to adapt to continuous change.

We know that periods of major technological change, such as the Industrial Revolution or the Information Revolution we are now undergoing, have major effects on how nations create and distribute wealth. During these times of economic and social change, the most vulnerable groups such as children can be adversely affected.

A second, related issue involves new research which shows that children raised in low- and even middle-income families don't enjoy the same health and educational achievement as children in higher income families. Studies show that the greater the gap in incomes, the greater the difference in the well-being and potential between rich and poorer children. Economies, such as Japan's, which have a relatively narrow gap between rich and poor have done better than economies with a wider income gap, including Canada and the United States.

These findings based on economic and social analysis suggest that societies which both invest the most in human capital and reduce inequities of income among the population will enjoy the greatest economic success. Investing in human capital begins by providing an environment that fosters healthy, happy children who are ready and eager to learn.

Canada's economic future and prosperity 10 and 20 years from now will depend on how well the country grapples with these issues. Fortunately, recent research has led to some powerful new discoveries. These include the importance of early brain development to later competence and coping skills, and the critical role of high quality social environments in providing the stimulation and nurturing that children require to fully develop. These new findings, which are summarized in this book, equip us with the know-how to develop strategies that best nurture optimal child development — at a time when it is most needed.

THE "CHIPS FOR NEURONS" REVOLUTION

Children today are growing up in a world of rapid change. We are living through one of those transformations, which happen from time to time in history. Like the Industrial Revolution which transformed economies and social institutions two centuries ago, Canada and other Western societies are

"The 'chips for neurons' revolution brings unprecedented opportunities to Canada. There is now the capacity to make large amounts of knowledge available immediately to individuals linked together through electronic networks without geographic or political barriers. A health care professional located in a remote part of Canada (and much of Canada is remote) can consult with leading experts across the world in less time than a specialist can consult with another specialist just down the hall. The potential of collaborative work possible using information technology could address our most complex scientific, economic and social problems. But we need to invest in a future workforce that has the capacity to be in command of this technology, not in its servitude." E1

Fraser Mustard

undergoing a major change, called the Information Revolution or Electronic Age. It is having a powerful effect on our economy, political systems and social institutions. These developments constitute a change that is often called the "chips for neurons" revolution.

If Canada is to meet the challenges and exploit the opportunities presented by this change, it must invest in its citizens — its "human capital." Natural resources and physical infrastructure will certainly not be enough for a society to prosper in the electronic age. Building human capital means creating social and physical environments that support optimal development for all children in order to raise young people who are healthy, competent and able to cope with challenges and change. This is a key part of the challenge of maintaining social cohesion, trust and stability.

Social cohesion means that individuals are woven together with shared values, purposes and goals. A high degree of social cohesion is powerful in pulling individuals together to face challenges and adversity such as war or natural disasters. At other times, national projects like building a railway across Canada or constructing our social safety net have been the glue of social cohesion in Canada. Social cohesion and stability create the kinds of neighbourhoods and communities that nurture and support children and youth.

Technological change brings new opportunities for people but also serious risks. Upheavals and disruptions that come with a major technological revolution tear at a society's cohesion and create instability. There are often disruptions in the families and neighbourhoods where children grow up. These have negative effects on child development and on the health and well-being of the entire population. Technological changes hit the most vulnerable members of a society the hardest. In our society the most vulnerable members are mothers and children.

The challenge for developed countries is to maintain stable, cohesive societies in the face of complex institutional change and shifts in employment that accompany major technological innovations. New knowledge about the factors affecting human development, particularly the importance of early childhood, gives societies the opportunity to meet the challenge. Our expanded understanding of the factors that influence the development of competence and coping skills early in life allows us to handle this change better now than in the past.

Our challenge is to provide the kind of quality environments that children need to develop fully. Our knowledge of the factors that influence human development early in life, as outlined in *Our Promise to Children*, allows us to make the most of this opportunity. Along with this opportunity, however, come serious risks.

IMPACT OF OUR CHANGING ECONOMY ON JOBS AND INCOME

Like earlier changes such as the Industrial Revolution and the transition to electricity, today's technological changes called the "chips for neurons" revolution pose challenges to society's ability to maintain quality social environments for all children. We know now that the changes brought on by the Information Age will be profound and will affect our labour markets, employment practices and social stability. Here are some of the problems we are facing.

— Canada's economy — in particular the capacity to create jobs — has not yet adjusted to the current technological changes. ❷ Because our wealth-creating capacity is still in the process of adjusting to the technological changes, we have not created the jobs that the new economy could

It's instructive to look back on the earlier period of technological change — the Industrial Revolution. The Industrial Revolution was a major technological change that influenced Western societies. During this time, fossil fuels such as coal were harnessed as energy sources. Human, animal and water power were replaced by steam engines. In a few decades, economies that had been focused on farms and villages became centred on industrial cities and factories. This had a major impact on economies and on social institutions from families to governments.

As Rosenberg and Birdzell point out in How the West Got Rich, **E2** the Industrial Revolution led to vastly improved levels of prosperity in Western countries. Improvements in the prosperity of societies led to improvements in the quality of life over time for individuals. The capacity to produce goods with less labour contributed to the end of serfdom and slavery. Increased opportunities for women and the creation of states with universal suffrage also developed over time.

In his 1993 Nobel prize lecture, Robert Fogel noted that this technological change led to vast improvements in the health of Western countries, primarily by creating more prosperous citizens and improvements in the well-being of children. He emphasized that the improvement in the health and well-being of the populations was a substantial factor in the future economic growth that followed the Industrial Revolution. Fogel's historical research concludes that the improvement in the lives of children had significant effects on the incidence of chronic disease in later life. **E3**

The Industrial Revolution had many downsides, particularly during the initial periods of change and adjustment. People were displaced from their means of earning a living. Long-standing communities disintegrated as workers were displaced from manual types of employment. Rapid growth in urban centres without adequate resources led to increased criminal activity and the creation of an underclass which was destitute, isolated and with no means of support.

But as societies learned to adapt to the new technology, they began to use it to improve the living conditions and the quality of life. In countries such as France and England, mortality rates began to drop substantially around 1840. Better nutrition, made possible by increased use of new technology in food production, led to better fed children and adults who lived longer.

Two simple observations, applicable to changes we are undergoing today, can be made about that earlier period of transformation. First, greater prosperity led to improved child health and indeed improved overall health. Second, improved population health was a major contribution to the economic growth that followed the Industrial Revolution. 🄱 Like the Industrial Revolution, the Information Revolution also holds out promise of a "virtuous circle" of greater prosperity and improved health and human development.

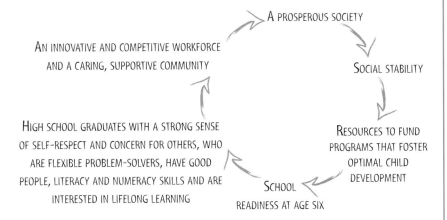

The Virtuous Circle: The Interrelationship Between Economic and Social Goals

A PROSPEROUS SOCIETY

AN INNOVATIVE AND COMPETITIVE WORKFORCE AND A CARING, SUPPORTIVE COMMUNITY

SOCIAL STABILITY

HIGH SCHOOL GRADUATES WITH A STRONG SENSE OF SELF-RESPECT AND CONCERN FOR OTHERS, WHO ARE FLEXIBLE PROBLEM-SOLVERS, HAVE GOOD PEOPLE, LITERACY AND NUMERACY SKILLS AND ARE INTERESTED IN LIFELONG LEARNING

RESOURCES TO FUND PROGRAMS THAT FOSTER OPTIMAL CHILD DEVELOPMENT

SCHOOL READINESS AT AGE SIX

This diagram was prepared by Gillian Doherty, based on the work of Dan Offord. Source: *Zero to Six: The Basis for School Readiness*, 1997, R-97-8E. Ottawa: Applied Research Branch, Strategic Policy, Human Resources Development Canada.

provide. At the same time, the replacement of low-level, routine work with electronic devices has threatened many jobs and decreased job security.

— **Overall, family incomes are stagnant, and many young families have seen their incomes decline.** ❸ This situation, combined with changes in family structure, has affected children. An increase of lone-parent families, led largely by women (often under age 40) marks a steady social change. Almost 17 percent of Canada's children live in a lone-parent family, and the group of Canadians in the greatest financial difficulty tends to be lone-parent mothers with young children. Meanwhile, two-parent families with

The Gradient in Health and Education Outcomes ❹

Low Birth Weight by Income Level
Canada, 1986

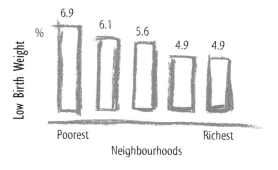

Health outcomes at birth are related to the family's socioeconomic status. Poor and middle-income families in Canada are at higher risk of having a low birth weight baby than richer families.

Literacy Scores for Canadian Children Ages 16–25

1994 International Literacy Study

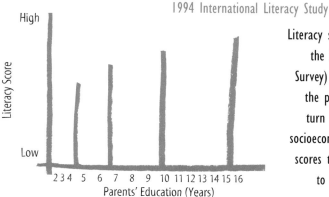

Literacy scores (based on data from the International Adult Literacy Survey) are related to the level of the parents' education, which in turn is a predictor of a family's socioeconomic status. Youth literacy scores tend to increase in relation to parents' educational levels.

young children frequently need two incomes to try to compensate for falling income levels. Both groups face increased stress during this time of change. In most two-parent families, both parents work in the labour force for an increasing number of hours each week.

— **We have not been able to sustain the same level of labour force incomes as we did from the end of the Second World War into the 1970s.** ❹ In the 1970s, the bottom half of our society (determined by income) received 75 percent of their income from employment and 25 percent from government transfer payments (social assistance, employment insurance and family allowances). In 1992, less than 35 percent of the same group's income comes from work. The rest comes from transfer payments. Over the past decade, Canada used transfer payments to maintain the level of income equity (or size of the gap between the richest and poorest groups). Transfer payments are dropping in Canada, so we can expect that, barring major policy changes, the total family income in poorer families will decline and the gap between the richest and poorest will widen.

A further widening of that income gap — a steeper gradient — will only make it more difficult to sustain high quality social environments which are necessary for optimal child development.

DISTRIBUTION OF INCOME: THE GRADIENT

The pressures widening the gap between the top and bottom income groups in Canada are disturbing — for developed countries, overall health is better the narrower the gap between top and bottom income groups. There is also evidence that a narrower gap has other social benefits.

Within every country there is a gradient in income that is related to a gradient in life expectancy, health and educational attainment. As the graphs on the opposite page show, there's a slope — at the top are the people with the highest income, at the bottom are the poorest. With each step up the slope you gain not just income — health and education outcomes also improve. (Health outcomes usually include mortality and disease rates; educational outcomes include early readiness to learn, academic achievement and high school dropout rates.)

The link between income and health is not merely about a contrast between deprivation suffered by the poor and abundance enjoyed by the rich. Middle-class people, with proportionately adequate food and shelter, also have worse health prospects than the rich. [5]

The gradient is apparent in many health indicators, one example being low birth weight statistics. Low birth weight is an indicator of early developmental problems for babies (see Chapter 6). Data from the Manitoba Centre for Health Policy and Evaluation shows that mothers on each step of the income ladder have babies with higher birth weights, on average, than mothers on the step below. [6] This comparison suggests that modest- and middle-income Canadians are at risk of raising children who are less healthy and resilient than Canadians who have high incomes. In fact, the actual number of children facing difficulties is far greater within middle-income groups than within the lowest or poorest groups.

In Canada, the National Longitudinal Survey of Children and Youth also found a gradient for the results of math computation tests and teachers' assessments of how well children were doing in various subjects. Both the math tests and teachers' assessments showed that poor children fared worst in schools, while children from higher incomes did the best. When children in elementary schools are ranked by socioeconomic group, children in the bottom fifth income group are more likely to be placed in remedial education classes. Teachers are more likely to rate children from the richest families as doing very well in their schoolwork. [7]

Comparisons between countries also shed some light on the impact of income gradients. The difference in scores between poorer Canadian children and richer Canadian children are less than the differences found among American children. In the Canadian study, differences in socioeconomic status accounted for only 5 percent of the differences in scores, while differences in socioeconomic status accounted for 10 to 15 percent of the differences in scores in the United States. [8]

However, other countries do much better than Canada. Robbie Case of the University of Toronto's Institute of Child Study points to mathematical scores of children 13 years old in Canada compared to those in the

United States and Japan. The achievement of children on math tests shows sharp differences in distinct socioeconomic groups for American children, smaller differences for Canadian children, and very little difference among Japanese children except for those at the peak. The Japanese scores are also much higher, on average. **9**

There are several explanations for the differences, rooted in the characteristics of each society. But it is noteworthy that there is much greater income equity in Japan: the gap between the rich and poor is smaller, nor are there as many Japanese in each group at either end of the income spectrum. The income gradient is relatively flat. Not coincidentally, Japan has also experienced the greatest involvement in overall population health in history during the last half-century, during which it has also become one of the most successful economies in the world.

Math Scores of 13-Year-Old Children in Relation to Socioeconomic Status **E5**

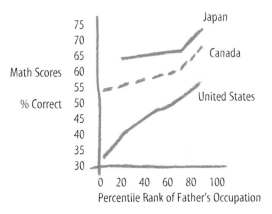

The father's socioeconomic status (as indicated by occupation) is a factor in predicting a child's math scores. Note that the math scores of children in Japan are higher than those in Canada and the United States. In addition, the gap between the scores of children in the lowest and highest socioeconomic groups is smaller in Japan. By contrast, the United States has the greatest gap between children's performance in the lowest and highest socioeconomic groups. Overall, the American scores are lower than the Canadian and Japanese scores.

The findings of British scientist Richard Wilkinson seem to confirm that a society that favours equity of incomes is healthier. The nations of the world with the longest life expectancy are not the wealthiest of the developed countries, but those with the smallest spread of incomes between the richest and the poorest, and the smallest proportions of the population living in relative poverty. ⑩

A question arising from this research is "what factors account for the link between health and income?" One theory suggests that having a feeling of control over one's life may be one important link. The poor in Canada may not be as poor in strictly material terms as the poor in a developing nation. But Wilkinson says the "social meanings" ⑪ people attach to the inferior living conditions and how they feel about themselves affect their health. In addition, a variety of studies have shown the impact of psychosocial factors on people's health.

Workplace studies in the United States, Sweden, Germany and Britain found that the three most important health-related aspects of the work environment are the amount of control people have over their work, the pressure of work and the social support they get from colleagues. Wilkinson suggests these factors probably apply to home and family circumstances as well as to working conditions. ⑩ Poorer people often have less control, higher stress and less social support. Economic hardship reduces people's ability to fulfil their roles as breadwinner or homemaker and can lead to depression, with its attendant feelings of isolation and helplessness.

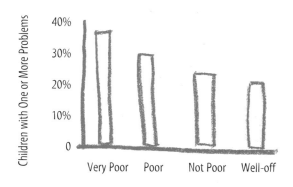

Children with One or More Problems

40%
30%
20%
10%
0

Very Poor   Poor   Not Poor   Well-off

Frequency of Problems among Children by Family Income Level ⑥

As children's family income increases, they are less likely to have an emotional or behavioural problem, difficulties in relating to others or to have repeated a grade in school.

This kind of research on the income gradient indicates that Canadian children face serious challenges, made more urgent by the current technological revolution. It also illustrates that income and social status are among the most powerful influences on the development of children. Children in the lower parts of the gradient may not only experience problems of later performance in the education system but also health problems in later life, including mental health disorders. In fact, low income works like a toxic substance. The higher the poverty level and the longer the duration of poverty, the more negative the consequences on cognitive development. Poverty is toxic to children's development, just as cigarette smoking is toxic to the health of young people and adults.

These educational and health difficulties are not only problems for the individual, they translate into a burden and loss of human capital for our society. This is not a problem of "us versus them" — the solution involves and benefits all groups.

According to Clyde Hertzman, "efforts to improve the conditions that maximize early development for all children will impact on those living in the worst conditions. Moreover, it is clear from international and interprovincial comparisons of child development that improving the conditions at the low end of the socioeconomic spectrum helps improve them at the upper end as well." **E7**

PREPARING FOR THE FUTURE TODAY

We are living in a new kind of world. The demands on the economy have changed. The demands on families have changed. The demands on social systems have changed. Social norms have changed. New technologies are transforming how we work, how we communicate, how we live. And these changes are happening at a remarkable pace.

What this tells us is that we cannot go on doing what we have always been doing and expect to get the same return — a relatively healthy, productive and prosperous population.

There are new and powerful forces at work that require new and creative responses. The challenges and opportunities are substantial. Societies that can cope will be ones that are able to integrate new knowledge on human development into policies and practices. Canada faces two equally pressing challenges if we are to thrive as a nation — we must build the new economy that creates wealth from ideas and innovation, and we must sustain the healthy social environment that is best for human development. Not one or the other, but both.

The Canadian economy will prosper in this new age to the extent that it can maximize the number of children who grow up in an environment that equips them to meet these emerging challenges. There are a number of potential creative solutions. For example, as the primary source of the wealth-creating capacity, the trade and business service sectors would continue to replace the wealth we need to sustain a society with a high standard of living. But as a result of technological changes, this sector may employ fewer people. The new job opportunities could well be created by investments in the sectors that support child development, such as early childhood care and education, supports to young parents, and education.

As we currently struggle with enormous technological, economic and social changes, our mission is not only to ensure that our children survive the transition but that they thrive. Taking care of those who fall off the track is not enough anymore. How Canada handles this task will determine how well we do as a society.

The rest of this book outlines what we can do to enhance a growing child's environment. The next chapter outlines four determinants of optimal child development — protection, relationships, opportunities and hope, and community. As a society, we need to create environments for children that support the development of health, competence and coping skills, and which make possible the full participation of children in a new world shaped by the "chips for neurons" revolution. Anything less will compromise Canada's potential and promise.

ENDNOTES

1. Keating & Mustard, 1996, p.8
2. OECD, 1995
3. Canadian Council on Social Development, 1996
4. Picot & Myles, 1996
5. Hertzman & Mustard, 1997
6. Mustard, 1993
7. Human Resource Development Canada & Statistics Canada, 1997
8. Willms, 1996A
9. Case, 1997
10. Wilkinson, 1994
11. Wilkinson, 1994, p. 70

EXHIBIT ENDNOTES

E1. Mustard, personal interview
E2. Rosenberg & Birdzell, 1986 in Frank & Mustard, 1994
E3. Fogel, 1994 in Frank & Mustard, 1994
E4. Adapted from Wilkins, Sherman and Best, 1991 in CICH, 1994A
    Adapted from OECD and Statistics Canada, 1995 in Willms, 1997
E5. Case, 1997
E6. Offord & Lipman, 1996
E7. Hertzman, interview

SECTION II
WHAT MAKES A DIFFERENCE TO CHILDREN'SDEVELOPMENT?

The Four Determinants of Optimal Child Development

Chapter 5
WHAT ALL CHILDREN NEED:
Four Determinants of Optimal Child Development

What do children need? There's no easy answer to this question. Every child is different. They have strengths and weaknesses, talents and limitations. They begin life in different circumstances.

But there are certain things children generally need in order to develop. These developmental needs are the things a country will want to provide for its children. Each is a kind of doorway that children need to step through on their way to becoming adults. A door is a good symbol. It represents opportunity. For some children, doors swing open easily. For others, the doors are heavy. And in some cases, the door is stuck shut. Adults in society sometimes need to turn the knob or push the door open.

DOORWAYS

There's a large carving at the entrance to the Sir William Macdonald Elementary School in Vancouver's inner city. It was done by a master carver, an elder of the Aboriginal community, whose grandchild attended the school. The eagle and the two wolves are said to be guarding the place where the children are. The doorway is also meant to show the neighbourhood that this is a place that respects and celebrates community culture.

THE FOUR DETERMINANTS

Children need food, clothing, shelter, love, toys, stimulation, opportunities to learn — and the list goes on. Researchers call these the determinants of healthy development. It's helpful to sort those needs into categories and group the determinants into four key areas. These are not the only ones that could be chosen, but there's substantial support in many studies for selecting them. The studies do not all come to the same conclusions, but taken together they point in general directions.

The "four determinants" draw attention to what the research shows is most likely to help most children. Here's a quick rundown:

~ **Protection** — Children need protection from harm and neglect. Babies and young children are physically dependent on adults for their safety, for their very survival. Children need good nutrition to grow and to learn. Their mothers need an adequate diet during pregnancy. But adolescence should be protected, too, as a time to learn responsibility and meet challenges within safe limits. It should be a time to receive guidance in negotiating the transition from dependence to independence.

~ **Relationships** — Human beings need other people to thrive, biologically and socially. Children's developmental potential is supported or diminished by the care and attention they receive from their parents, friends, relatives, neighbours, teachers and other caring adults.

~ **Opportunity and hope** — Children and young people need opportunities to play, to explore, to love, to learn, to listen, to share, to be heard, to work, to take and to give back. They need to learn skills, explore their interests and test their abilities. Opportunities enable children and young people to build self-esteem and sustain hope for the future.

~ **Community** — Most children grow up in a family. Families need support networks around them; they thrive or flounder within communities. Communities flourish within society. Societies need a strong sense of community and social cohesion to foster the conditions that make for optimal child development.

This chapter discusses, in a general way, how these determinants work. The subsequent four chapters will explore each of these topics in turn. As you can see, the dividing lines between the determinants are not always firm: there is some overlap between material discussed in each.

OPENING THE DOORS

There are many doorways that children need to pass through on the way to adulthood. These "determinants" tend to *lead* to good development for children, but they do not necessarily *make* children healthy and well-adjusted. For example, the love and support of parents and other adults, and the friendship and understanding of siblings and friends are extremely important to a growing child. A child who has such strong and loving relationships is more likely to do well than one who does not, but these relationships do not guarantee a good outcome.

> *Opening doors for children leads to good outcomes for children and youth. Good outcomes can be defined in many ways, for example:*
> C — *coping, caring, capable, creative, confident*
> H — *happy, healthy, hopeful*
> I — *interested, industrious, included*
> L — *loving, learning, laughing*
> D — *determined, dedicated*
> R — *resourceful, responsible, respected*
> E — *exploring, empathetic, equal*
> N — *nurtured and nurturing*

A determinant can also be viewed as an indicator or "marker" of healthy development. If you find that a child is growing up safe, well nourished and well nurtured, for example, it can be a sign that the child is getting the chances needed to develop to full potential.

If these doorways are open, Canada's children will have a better chance of thriving than if they are closed.

These determinants do not eliminate stress or risk. But if they are present across all environments in which children live, it will help them cope better with life's challenges.

To work best, these doorways must be opened early, and stay open.

Good things that happen early — particularly during sensitive periods of brain development in the first few years of life — provide a basis for good development later. This does not mean that early nurturing makes children problem-proof. A good start must have a good follow-through, or the developmental gains made in early life may be wasted later. These determinants operate over time, across the developmental cycle. Children need ongoing support as they go through the different phases of growing up.

A doorway that is closed at one time in a child's life may be opened in another.

It's important not to write off children who get off to a bad start developmentally. Research shows that children who begin life in difficult circumstances can bounce back later if they get what they missed early in life — it's just more difficult and expensive.

A doorway that is closed in one aspect of a child's life may be opened in another.

If there's something missing in one environment, children may find it in another. For example, parental expectations can influence a young person's motivation in school. But teachers and other school staff who show a personal interest in a child's well-being and encourage the achievement of life goals can make a difference for a child living in a troubled household. Community resources like free recreational and arts programs can provide opportunities for children whose families live in poverty. However, as the next point illustrates, it's hard for good things in one environment to compensate for a lot of bad things in others.

If there are multiple doorways, a child will be more likely to find a way to reach his or her potential.

These determinants seem to work best if they are reinforced over time and in a number of environments.

One positive cannot be expected to make up for many negatives. A local recreation program may provide opportunities for children to learn new skills, make friends and build self-confidence, but cannot by itself overcome the negative effects of an unstable family, poverty and an indifferent school environment.

In contrast, a dynamic school that involves parents — together with neighbourhood groups willing to work on behalf of children, and a system that supports community initiative and social investments in children — provides a combination of positive forces that reinforce each other, offering better opportunities for all children to thrive.

These doorways represent an alternative route for society.

Society puts a lot of resources into dealing with social and economic problems that arise largely because children have not had the chances they need to grow up healthy and well-adjusted. Treating problems is expensive and often unsuccessful. The cost of wasted lives is enormous in both human and economic terms.

For example, there's a great deal of concern about youth violence. The behavioural problems that show up in teenagers, however, didn't occur overnight. It's far more successful to support parents and young children early in their development, helping them deal with anger and aggressive tendencies. Unless we adopt an approach that promotes optimal child development from the earliest age, we will keep needing more child psychiatrists, more youth detention centres, more school security.

Opening doorways to healthy development for children is a way of strengthening Canada's pool of "human capital," which is widely believed to be our key asset in the global economy during a time of economic transformation.

THE WORK OF THE NATIONAL CRIME PREVENTION COUNCIL: SUPPORTING A "DETERMINANTS OF OPTIMAL CHILD DEVELOPMENT" APPROACH

"There are many opportunities at various stages in a child's life to help ensure that children develop competence and social responsibility. The earlier children receive the supports they need, however, the greater the chance they will develop healthy and productive lifestyles.

What do children need to develop and behave in more pro-social ways?

Children must be free from the risk factors related to poverty. Effective prenatal care and nurturing parents help promote babies with secure attachments. The physical safety and emotional well-being of children are protected by caring families who understand and respond to the developmental needs of their children. Security and social responsibility are fostered by parents who are actively involved in raising their children and providing effective discipline. Opportunities for exploring and learning through educational and social activities encourage the acquisition of skills that children need to meet the challenges of school. The right kind of school experience improves outcomes for children. Finally, supportive communities help buffer negative influences and strengthen protective factors in the lives of children." **E1**

CONCLUSION

It's a touching image. What adult hasn't seen a young child struggling outside a school or a store to pull open a heavy door to get inside. The natural reaction for any adult is to reach out and open that door for the child. But the struggles that most children face every day aren't as easy to see as a physical door. Helping is tougher than just grabbing a handle. However, the instinct to give a child a helping hand remains. The spirit of not wanting to see children shut out is right. The challenge is to learn to see what doorways are closed for which children and how best to get them open. All partners in society — families, communities, employers and governments — share the responsibility for getting these doors open and helping children pass through them.

EXHIBIT ENDNOTE
E1. National Crime Prevention Council, 1996

Chapter 6
CHILDHOOD SHOULD BE PROTECTED:
The First Determinant of Optimal Child Development

Young human beings are helpless for longer than the young of any other animal species. This lengthy period of dependence places a lot of responsibility on parents, relatives, neighbours and the community to protect children. But it pays off. Protecting childhood as a special time to play, explore and learn has allowed humans to develop creativity and reasoning. Indeed, the long childhood of human beings has been called one of the keys to the cultural evolution of the species.

A WEB OF PROTECTION

Children need to be safeguarded from the pressures of adult life until they have the maturity and resilience to handle them. Young children shouldn't have to face chronic loneliness, fear or worry. Adolescents should be guided toward responsibility and independence, and away from dangerous choices such as drugs, unprotected sex, and drinking and driving. Parents are on the front lines of protection for their children, but they cannot be watching everywhere all the time. Other parts of society also have responsibilities to protect children.

One way society tries to protect childhood is through laws and regulations. Children are required to go to school. Schools are regulated and child care programs are licensed. Special car seats are required for small children. Some provinces put limits on drivers' licences for new, young drivers and require children to wear bicycle helmets. Alcohol consumption is regulated by age. It is illegal to sell cigarettes to children. Child welfare agencies have the legal authority to take children from their homes if they are endangered by abuse or neglect. Children who get into trouble are treated more leniently than adults by the law and courts.

Sometimes seemingly simple regulations do a lot of good. Requiring child-proof caps on medicines and dangerous household products is likely far more effective at preventing accidental poisoning than campaigns to remind parents to put dangerous substances in locked cupboards.

Laws and regulations are not enough, though. For one thing, resources will never be sufficient to ensure adequate enforcement. The protection of children ultimately rests with the wider community providing the supports that not all parents, and no single institution like a child welfare authority, are able to offer.

Neighbours who watch out for kids going to and from school and the playground can help improve security and relieve parental anxiety. Friends can provide emotional support to families. Professionals, such as doctors and teachers, must be on the lookout for signs of abuse and family violence, and report them. Manufacturers of clothes and toys should hold themselves to high standards of safety.

The emphasis on protection may differ depending on the community. In one neighbourhood, providing a crossing-guard at a busy intersection near the elementary school or launching an anti-drinking and driving campaign aimed at teenagers may be a big local safety issue. In another community, the issues may be preventing abuse and feeding children who come to school hungry.

A caring community will provide safe playgrounds, good child care, child-friendly public buildings, parent-child resource centres and other support for parents, such as opportunities to learn positive parenting skills. Schools must be involved in their communities and communities involved in their schools.

Protection is broader than just keeping children away from dangers. Children also have to be protected from want. They have to be protected from hunger, poverty and ill health.

Protection, as a determinant of healthy child development, is fundamental. Children can be hurt, damaged for life or die if they are not protected. Protecting childhood as a sheltered period for development also says something important about how much we value the raising of the next generation. Protecting children must start in the very beginning — in the womb.

EVEN BEFORE BIRTH

If our society believes in protecting childhood, we have to start with support for pregnant women. Mothers need an adequate diet during pregnancy to nourish themselves and their babies. Pregnant women who are below average weight or who do not gain enough weight during pregnancy are more likely to have low birth weight babies, that is, under 2.5 kilograms or 5.5 pounds. Some of these babies may suffer health problems, including long-term disability; others may die.

Low birth weight is not just a matter of chance. Low birth weight rates in Canada are higher for those who are poor than for Canadians with middle or upper incomes. About 22,000 low birth weight babies were born in 1990, out of about 405,000 live births (5 percent). This proportion has not dropped much in recent years. Compared to other countries, Canada's rate of low birth weight is in the middle range for developed countries — lower than the United States and Britain, but higher than France and Sweden. ❶

Two groups of women are most at risk for inadequate weight gain during pregnancy — the poor and teenagers. These women often can't afford the right food during pregnancy and sometimes lack skills for food budgeting, buying and cooking. ❷ A mother's diet has an impact on more than the baby's physical health since the child's ability to learn can also be affected. Diet supplements for pregnant women who might otherwise be poorly nourished are likely to contribute to improved learning skills when their children go to school. ❸

Targeted programs can have a highly significant impact on low birth weight rates. The Montreal Diet Dispensary is one of the oldest of several active programs across the country which try to improve the health of mothers and infants with nutritional counselling, food supplements and other support during pregnancy. The Dispensary, started in the 1960s to improve the health of poor women and their babies, combines nutritional supplements with social supports and suggestions for lifestyle improvement for pregnant women. A comparison of the weights of babies born to women before and after they started participating in the program showed the rate of low birth weights is cut in half. ❷

In Vancouver and Toronto, programs to foster the "Healthiest Babies Possible" have been run by public health departments for many years. These programs provide health and nutrition counselling, milk supplements and other supports to high-risk pregnant women.

A 1996 report from the Toronto Healthiest Babies Possible program serving disadvantaged pregnant women said the rate of low birth weight among its clients has been cut nearly in half over the past 10 years, from 11.2 percent to 5.9 percent. ❹

The Toronto program had other benefits, such as increasing the number of mothers who breastfeed. After birth, breastfeeding provides infants with nutritional advantages and greater resistance to illness, infections and allergies. The proportion of breastfeeding mothers in the Toronto program increased from 57 percent in 1987-90 to 84 percent in 1993-95.

Many of the women in the Toronto program did not have enough money for an adequate diet and some were also concerned about body image and weight gain during pregnancy. With help, which included coupons for milk, their diets improved. Virtually all the women who had initially been eating fewer than three meals a day improved their eating habits. Smoking is also known to contribute to low birth weight and here too there were gains: the majority (75 percent) of the smokers in the program quit or cut down.

Social supports are also important to a healthy pregnancy. About half of the women attended prenatal group programs and the program's home visiting teams, which included a dietitian and public health nurse, found that many of these women were stressed by poor housing and financial problems. A home-visit program, combined with food supplements, can do a lot. Clearly, however, it can't be expected to address all the socioeconomic stresses on families.

SUBSTANCE ABUSE DURING PREGNANCY

Substance abuse by a pregnant woman can be devastating to her child. Fetal alcohol syndrome (FAS) was first described in the 1970s. The syndrome involves serious brain damage and is estimated to be the leading cause of developmental handicaps in Canada. Some children born with the less severe fetal alcohol effects (FAE) have normal intelligence but display a range of behavioural problems and learning disabilities. It is not known exactly how much alcohol causes damage. The problems of FAS and FAE are particularly acute in some remote rural communities and some Aboriginal communities. **5**

Research findings on the impact of smoking on prenatal, infant and early child development are very definitive. **6** During pregnancy, smoking increases the chance of a miscarriage, stillbirth and death of the newborn. It also increases problems with the placenta, such as breaking away from the uterus wall or excessive bleeding. Smoking increases the risk of premature birth and reduces the newborn's potential birth weight. A pregnant mother's use of tobacco is the major environmental risk to healthy births in North America.

Newborns, infants and young children are also harmed by adult usage of tobacco products. Second-hand smoke increases coughs, respiratory infections and asthma. It is particularly harmful to children who are born at a very low birth weight.

FEEDING YOUNG BODIES AND MINDS

Nutrition is one of the most powerful factors in the growth and development of infants and children. A healthy diet is important throughout life, but it is vital in the early years. We associate severe malnutrition among children with poor countries and situations of famine and war, but even peaceful, developed countries such as Canada have children who are suffering the effects of undernourishment. A symptom of this is the fact that food banks have become a common institution in Canada. They help feed thousands of families who are working at low-paid jobs or living on social assistance — families without enough money for adequate meals, plus rent, utilities and clothing.

Many children are coming to class so hungry they can't learn and schools across Canada have responded by starting breakfast, lunch or snack programs. Undernourished children get sick more often and miss school. They tend to be less physically active and more tired, less attentive and more apathetic. **7**

Adequate nutrition throughout childhood — not just in the first few months — is vital to development of a child's thinking and learning capacity. An inadequate diet may, in addition to impairing brain function, limit development in other ways. For example, one way in which poor nutrition seems to affect intellectual development is through its effect on overall health. If motor development is delayed by poor health, the child's exploration of the surrounding environment may be limited. An inadequate diet may also leave children weakened, with little or no energy to socialize with others or to learn. **8**

Nutrition programs for children can promote healthy development and increase the benefits of education. Well-fed kids are more likely to develop to their potential and to get more out of school. Of course, nutrition programs by themselves are not the answer to reducing the systemic problem of poverty and its negative effects on children — just as home visiting and food supplements for pregnant women cannot remove the stress of poor housing and poverty. But studies have found that disadvantaged children who are better fed and whose mothers ate better during pregnancy achieve more in school than their disadvantaged peers, and that the advantage of improved nutrition increases with every additional year of schooling. Still, these children don't do as well as children who come from more comfortable economic circumstances. **8**

ABUSE AND NEGLECT: A SOCIAL FAILURE

Abuse and neglect of children have long-lasting consequences for its victims. Children who suffer a history of abuse are more likely to have psychiatric and other health problems. They are also more likely to have trouble at school and drop out early. Children with a history of sexual abuse are more likely to become chemically dependent and to commit suicide. **9**

Violence and neglect during infancy and early years affect the brain's organization and chemical make-up, according to research conducted by Bruce Perry, with the CIVITAS Child Trauma Programs of the Baylor College of Medicine in Texas. **10**

Children who are severely abused or neglected may not learn how to control their feelings or behaviour. Changes in brain chemistry caused by

HEALING OURSELVES: A FIRST NATIONS INITIATIVE E1

A member of the Kajaet (Raven People) of the Hootchi Nation in the Yukon, Nechenechea Dakwa ul is coordinator of the Traditional Parenting Program, offered through the Skookum Jim Friendship Centre in Whitehorse, Yukon. The Skookum Jim Friendship Centre is a non-profit organization committed to a vision of bettering the spiritual, emotional, mental and physical well-being of First Nations people and other Yukoners in need. The Traditional Parenting Program is funded jointly by the Yukon government and the federal Community Action Program for Children.

Nechenechea Dakwa ul describes the background and mission of the program: "During the years of assimilation, the Government of Canada through the Indian Act removed thousands of First Nations children from their natural environment. These children were to be educated in mission schools, run by foreigners.... The schools' most profound impact was to all but eradicate our traditional lifestyle, and our unique culture based on principles and values which respected all of creation."

A report on First Nations education in the Yukon in 1986 concluded that one of the most significant factors hindering children's education was lack of parenting skills. "This was a direct result of the impact of the mission schools and the inability of families to adjust to a rapidly changing society. The lack of consistent parenting role models, being away from home and community, and eventually the loss of language which led to communication problems in families and in the communities, led also to other social problems...."

Another report in the 1980s investigating both children with chronic handicaps and children with FAS in the Yukon and northwest British Columbia, found that of the 586 children surveyed:

▲ about two-thirds were of First Nations ancestry;

▲ alcohol was involved in 59 percent of the pregnancies; and

▲ 176 children or 30 percent of the total study population had FAS/FAE.

"For years, the elders encouraged us to revisit our past as they recognized that young people were slowly losing touch with their cultures. With the gradual loss of these traditional ways, there has been an increase in the number of abused and neglected children as well as children born with FAS. They recognized, too, that it would have to be our responsibility to address our healing with respect to FAS/FAE. Our healing journey would have to begin with the basics, mainly because the basics are the skills we all but lost during the years of assimilation."

The Traditional Parenting Program of Skookum Jim is a prevention program aimed at First Nations families. Based on the advice of elders, who are key to the program, the development of parenting skills is directed toward whole families, not just pregnant women, to establish support for mothers and children. Elders — four women and four men — are the primary teachers. "We use the circle method of sharing, the circle being a place of respect and trust, where no one is above or below another," says Nechenechea Dakwa ul. Health professionals such as doctors, nurses, nutritionists and child development workers are invited to share their knowledge as well.

"It's ironic that as we move into the twenty-first century, our program is looking to a culture which is thousands of years old to assist us in addressing modern-day health issues and problems. This is what the Traditional Parenting Program is all about."

acute stress at key developmental periods may cause a child to react to stress with aggression or fear and withdrawal.

Children react to maltreatment in different ways. But in general, children who are neglected at a young age tend to withdraw, while children who are physically abused tend to become aggressive. It is important, however, not to generalize too much and the impact may vary according to the type of mistreatment and the age of the child.

Perry's research indicates that if a young child's brain is constantly or frequently in a state of arousal brought on by neglect and trauma, the actual chemical reaction of the brain to stress will or can be altered. This leads to an overdevelopment of anxiety and impulsive behaviour, combined with an underdevelopment of the ability to empathize and solve problems. These are the conditions that increase the chance of violent behaviour.

According to Perry, "Under all circumstances, the organ which allows the child victim to adapt to any violent trauma is the brain. Just as the brain is the organ that is the origin for the violent behaviours of the victimizer. How is it that the very neurobiological adaptations which allow the child to survive violence may, as the child grows older, result in an increased tendency to be violent?... In order to understand violence we need to understand the organization and functioning of its birthplace...the brain." [11]

STOPPING THE HURT

The prevalence in Canada of physical, sexual and emotional abuse and of chronic neglect is disturbingly high. Surveys in British Columbia indicated about 20 to 25 percent of Grades 8 and 9 students reported experiencing physical abuse. The Canadian Institute of Child Health reported that girls become increasingly vulnerable with age and they are almost twice as likely as boys to suffer physical abuse. By Grade 11, the incidence of sexual abuse is seven times higher among girls (28 percent) than boys (4 percent). [12]

A recent Ontario study from the Centre for Studies of Children at Risk finds that a third of adult males and a fifth of adult females report childhood physical abuse. The definition of physical abuse used by the study did not include any spanking or slapping, nor did it include shoving or grabbing if it rarely happened. Fathers, followed by mothers, were most often identified as the person committing physical abuse. The same study found 4 percent of men and 13 percent of women reported childhood sexual abuse. Other studies have shown that individuals providing retrospective accounts of child abuse tend to minimize or deny childhood experiences of abuse so that the actual prevalence of child abuse may be higher. **13**

Violence in the home is a huge social problem. Children in violent homes are deeply affected by the atmosphere of threat and fear even if they are not the ones assaulted.

Parents who are harsh and punitive are often depressed and isolated. A parent who has low self-esteem, lacks parenting skills, lives in poverty and lacks family support is more likely to mistreat children than a parent who is confident, has received parent education and adequate resources and support. **14** That doesn't mean the poverty or isolation cause abuse, just that they increase the risk that it will happen. Certainly, abuse and family violence occur in families in all economic categories, including

*Sometimes people get mad at me
and it makes me sad;
sometimes my father gets mad and
punches me.*

*Sometimes my parents fight,
they punch each other.
My friend, his parents fight too
their fights are badder,
they throw stuff around.*

*Sometimes my mother and father
get into big fights,
I try to break the fight up.*

*My father gets drunk sometimes.
Some people are messed up
when they're drunk.*

*They get into accidents or fights;
they run into cars or park
where there's no parking.*

*Sometimes they fall down when
they're drunk;
sometimes they get mad and kill
other people.*

*Sometimes they break valuable
stuff;
sometimes they break glass
butterflies.*

Philip, 7 years old,
participant in Growing Together,
St. Jamestown in downtown Toronto

the rich. Strategies to prevent and treat these social ills must be community-wide.

Whenever a case of child abuse ends in permanent injury or death, we usually blame the child welfare system for not intervening soon enough or in the right way. There have been some spectacular failures across the country. But child welfare workers, like the police, are fighting a rearguard action against a much larger social problem. That is why community awareness and action can make a difference.

The best approach, whenever possible, is to help support parents who need help raising their children. **15** Responsibility for preventing abuse must be shared by:

~ communities that work to prevent child abuse from occurring in the first place, by providing, for example, supports to parents such as parenting courses and family resource centres;

~ governments that provide adequate child welfare budgets for prevention and quality services;

~ neighbours who report abuse in their communities;

~ doctors, teachers and other professionals who learn to recognize abuse and effectively report it; and

~ mental health and social service workers who can support child welfare staff and provide quality evidence.

WINNIPEG PARENTING SUPPORT PROGRAM

In 1988, a research team from the School of Social Work at the University of Manitoba launched a demonstration project to see if improving supports for parents would reduce the risk of child abuse and neglect. They looked to the work of James Garbarino at Cornell University who, along with others, has argued that rather than putting all our resources into one-to-one rehabilitation of abused children, we should be working with communities to create support networks for parents and reinforce pro-child values to prevent abuse. **16**

Workers with the Neighbourhood Parenting Support Project talked to parents in two downtown low-income neighbourhoods. The interviewers found that a majority of parents were concerned about crime, gangs, vandalism and drunks wandering the neighbourhood. They worried about their children's safety going to and from school, and didn't think highly of the recreational and educational facilities and programs available to their children.

A lot of middle-income parents would probably express the same fears and concerns. But an important difference lies in the resources that well-off parents and neighbourhoods can call upon to respond to their worries. These low-income parents felt they had few people they could discuss personal problems with or go to for help. They were receiving minimal support from formal service systems, such as health, education and social services.

These low-income parents were also suffering considerable stress. Financial difficulties were severe. Life crisis stress (defined as major life changes such as family deaths, changes in marital status, personal injury or illness) was two to three times what parents living in similar communities reported in comparable studies. A majority of these parents experienced daily "blues" and longer depressive episodes. Project workers went into one of the neighbourhoods to help develop parent support networks — personal and professional, informal and formal — to help relieve some of the stress on families.

Both neighbourhoods started out in the summer of 1989 scoring twice as high as other communities tested on a scale that measures the risk of child maltreatment. In the summer of 1992, the "intervention" neighbourhood where the project operated showed a higher level of support among parents, lower levels of depression, a lower level of family violence and a lower level of risk for child maltreatment.

A note of caution: further analysis indicated that after the project ended, the parents experienced an upsurge in stress over life crisis events. The researchers suggested that the gains in risk reduction were fragile and required a longer-term sustained effort. **17**

The direct support provided to families by Winnipeg's Neighbourhood Parenting Support Project included:

■ identifying existing and potential social networks in the neighbourhood;

■ providing direct social support and coaching to parents in the areas of identifying and solving problems, networking skills, parenting skills, help-seeking skills, communication skills and support-giving skills;

■ strengthening informal helping and support available from other neighbours;

■ coordinating the resources available through the formal social service systems; and

■ increasing the family's capacity to work with social service personnel.

Parenting support workers also did other things, including participating in neighbourhood parents' meetings, supporting the development of a babysitting co-op, assisting a parent to develop a resource booklet and participating in a parent peer counselling program sponsored by a local health agency. (E2)

HEALTH AND OTHER CHALLENGES FACING YOUNG PEOPLE

Unprotected sex can kill. Illegal drugs that are readily available to the young are more harmful and more plentiful than ever. Youth unemployment is persistently and disproportionately high, leading to frustration and disillusionment.

Depression and other mental health problems seem to be increasing among young Canadians. Among children and youth aged 10 to 19, suicide is the second leading cause of death, after injuries which occur mostly from car accidents. Suicide among 15- to 19-year-olds has climbed substantially since the 1960s. (18)

Homosexual and bisexual male youths are more likely to commit or attempt to commit suicide than heterosexual males. A recent study conducted in Calgary suggests that they are almost 14 times more likely to attempt suicide. Christopher Bagley and Pierre Tremblay, the researchers who conducted the study, suggest that "the predominant reason for suicidality of these young males may be linked to the 'coming out' process occurring in a highly homophobic society." **19**

"Commissioners learned of the gravity of the suicide problem from the direct testimony of Aboriginal people. Their hearts are being broken and their resources depleted by the members who have tried to die. What hurts and frightens them the most are the deaths of the young.... Most concerning of all, we identified a strong possibility that the number of suicides among Aboriginal youth will rise in the next 10 to 15 years." **B**

Royal Commission on Aboriginal Peoples

ENCOURAGING YOUNG PEOPLE TO MAKE HEALTHY CHOICES

Helping young people make healthy choices is more important than ever, and perhaps more difficult than ever. Just lecturing kids is not good enough. Accurate, useful information is essential — on fitness, mental health, smoking, drinking, driving, illegal drugs, relationships, safe sex, parenting and more. But participation in community life and involvement with positive role models and other caring adults is even more vital.

Young people want to be heard. They want to be involved in decisions and solutions that affect their communities. The Adolescent Health Project, started in Antigonish, Nova Scotia in 1990 by a group of women concerned about the health needs of adolescents in their community, provides a model of how young people can participate in local projects.

"We brought with us the personal experience of being mothers, friends, neighbours and caregivers to adolescents," says Susan Jewkes, former director of the Adolescent Health Project. "We brought, as well, the pain of three recent teenage suicides in Antigonish; a growing awareness of increased adolescent sexual experimentation and activity and the health consequences of such behaviours; and a concern that our young people were facing pressures, dilemmas and decisions in a rapidly changing world that even we, as adults, had difficulty understanding." [20]

The women decided that one of the most important things to do was to talk to teenagers and hear their concerns. They did that. They wrote a report and local young people produced a video.

The group's goals include:

~ helping youth have a voice in the community;

~ enabling youth to identify their health needs and take responsibility for themselves;

~ providing opportunities for youth to work with the community; and

~ raising awareness and equipping adults and organizations to relate to and work with adolescents on health issues.

True to its principles, the direction, planning and implementation of the project is overseen by an Adolescent Advisory Committee, made up of an evolving group of young people. The first four years were focused mainly on substance use and abuse, mental wellness and relationships. Project activities have included health promotion events and projects; community forums and workshops; a community multicultural festival; media coverage; the development of a peer education program; and the formation of a local drug awareness committee. As a result of the Adolescent Health Project, youth have had a voice and influence on a range of issues in the community, including air quality and environmental health at the local high school, racism, violence and the development of health policy. "Teenagers have opinions and need to express them," said a young person in the community. "We see many things wrong in the world and if we are going to live in it, we need to be given the tools for change." [21]

According to Jewkes, "the family and community's role can be enhanced only through increased information, communication and support. It is how our community and its resources choose to support — or fail to support — our young people and their families that will determine if we can move toward solutions." [20]

A health promotion guide for teachers in British Columbia sums the challenge up well.

Health promotion is not:

▲ an aerobics class at noon;

▲ telling students not to smoke;

▲ a lecture on nutrition;

▲ giving information about school rules to parents and students.

Health promotion is:

▲ broad participation by students and teachers in school events that focus on active living;

▲ role modelling non-smoking and practising skills to resist peer pressure to smoke;

▲ making good food available in vending machines and school cafeterias and starting vegetable gardens as school projects;

▲ supporting mentor or peer counselling that models and rein-forces positive, caring relationships and training playground mediators. **E4**

IMPACT OF THE ENVIRONMENT ON CHILDREN'S HEALTH E5

Susceptibility of Children

Children are not small adults: they differ physiologically, developmentally and behaviourally from adults. These differences, determined primarily by their age and developmental stage, mean that children need specific protection from exposure to, and the effects of, environmental contaminants.

Adding to these effects are social and genetic factors. For instance, poverty can increase the negative effects of toxicants and, in some cases, children with genetic abnormalities have a lower capacity to overcome the effects of toxins.

Focusing on Protecting Children

Despite the documented differences in behaviour and physiology between children and adults, few studies have focused on children's health as it relates to environmental exposure. Some important issues are:

■ Environmental tobacco smoke is the number one indoor air problem for children.

■ Asthma in children has risen dramatically in the last decade.

■ Domestic use of pesticides has increased dramatically in the last decade, especially in urban settings.

■ Lead has unequivocally been proven to impair neurological development and function in children, but it is still found in soil, old paint, electronics and other household items.

■ There has been a threefold increase in new skin cancer cases from 1969 to 1996. Exposure to serious sunburns during childhood could potentially increase the development of melanoma later in life.

Recognizing the heightened sensitivity of the young, it's logical and appropriate to develop policies that protect the immediate and long-term safety of children. In May 1996, the Canadian Institute of Child Health (CICH) organized a national symposium on environmental contaminants and the implications for child health. Just one component of a multi-year strategy, the "What on Earth?" symposium provided a forum for Canadian and international experts to share ideas and develop a framework for action. For more information on the work of CICH and how to order its publications, refer to Appendix C.

Endnotes

1. Mustard, 1993
2. Hanvey, 1993
3. Doherty, 1992
4. Desjardins, 1996
5. Greene & Wilbee, 1992 in Hanvey, 1993
6. Morrison et al, 1993; Mainous & Hueston, 1994; Muscati et al, 1994; DiFranza & Lew, 1995
7. Toronto Board of Education, 1991
8. Brown & Politt, 1996
9. Canadian Institute of Child Health, 1994B
10. Perry, 1995
11. Perry, 1995, p. 5-6
12. McCreary Centre Society, 1993 in Canadian Institute of Child Health, 1994A
13. MacMillan et al, 1997
14. Beckwith, 1990
15. Steinhauer, interview
16. Garbarino, 1982; Lugtig & Fuchs, 1992
17. Fuchs, interview
18. Canadian Institute of Child Health, 1994A
19. Bagley & Tremblay, in press, p. 1
20. Jewkes, interview
21. Antigonish Adolescent Health Project, 1991, p. 5

Exhibit Endnotes

E1 Based on background community poster session presentation prepared by Nechenechea Dakwa ul for the National Symposium on Community Action for Children
E2 Lugtig & Fuchs, 1992
E3 Royal Commission on Aboriginal Peoples, 1995, p. 18
E4 Office of Health Promotion, B.C. Ministry of Health, 1991
E5 Based on interview with Denise Avard

Chapter 7

RELATIONSHIPS ARE KEY:
The Second Determinant of Optimal Child Development

We spend our whole lives relating to other people. The ability to form and maintain mutually supportive relationships with others is something every human being needs. Building relationships begins at birth with the love and nurturing of mothers, fathers, brothers and sisters. But children need and benefit from relationships outside the home. The extended family, child care workers, teachers, coaches and friends all contribute to the healthy development of children, simply by talking, listening and caring. People in the community who get involved can help children grow.

LEARNING TO LOVE

Children learn to love, to trust, to feel for others, through their experiences with the people around them. Secure relationships in the early years provide the foundation for building close relationships later in life.

As children grow, their experience with other people widens, and they learn from those experiences.

Is the person behind the counter at the corner store friendly or hostile because I'm a kid? Is there a neighbourhood dad or mom who will teach me to play hockey or soccer? Are there teachers who take an interest in what I'm like, not just how well I do in school? Will my friends teach me to dance? Is there a community centre or some place where I can go to make friends or just hang out? Will somebody give me a chance for work experience? Who cares about me?

Relationships between the child and other people, primarily parents, help to shape the child's view of himself or herself. Who am I? Am I someone who is loved and valued? Is the world around me scary or safe? Who is always there for me?

Supportive relationships buffer children against the slings and arrows that life hurls at them. Negative relationships, characterized by harshness or rejection, undermine trust and promote fear and anger in children. Over and over, the research emphasizes the importance of responsiveness and sensitivity of parents or other caregivers.

Children learn to relate; children relate to learn. They learn how to have warm and stable relationships as adults through their experiences with other people in childhood. At the same time, their intellectual growth evolves through their relationships with adults who guide their learning. ❶

The function that adults perform in helping children learn is called "scaffolding." ❶ Adults provide external support like a scaffold for children to build their cognitive or thinking abilities. As children get older, their peers who are more advanced in development may also help them move to higher skill levels.

Relationships matter whenever and wherever they occur. Beginning life with lots of parental love and attention is the best way to start. That's not always possible. But other people in the family or community can make a difference. Just one person who believes in a child and shows caring and respect can help make up for earlier insecurity in the family setting and assist a young person to become a fulfilled and responsible adult. ❷

Caring relationships in society need to be encouraged on two fronts. First, parents need to be supported in child rearing to help make sure they can provide good nurturing for their children. Second, children need support from other adults who are in a position to provide caring and to be role models of positive relationships.

EARLY ATTACHMENT HAS LONG-TERM IMPACTS

Behavioural studies of babies observed over many years have shown that the early attachment of an infant to a loving and responsive parent or other primary caregiver is vital to a child's healthy development. Researchers have spent thousands of hours studying the attachment of babies to their primary caregivers, usually their mothers. Attachment seems to be pre-programmed into the human personality. It is similar to the "imprinting" that occurs in some other species, notably birds. Birds will imprint on and follow the first caregiver they encounter after they come out of the egg. If the mother is not there, they will attach to whatever substitute is available, often a human being.

Attachment is more complex in humans. It is not as immediate after birth. But, as with other species, babies will develop attachment no matter what kind of care they receive. As long as there are no prolonged separations or serious threats to the babies' health, they will form an attachment to their main caregiver — the person who is their primary contact with the world — whether or not that person offers adequate or appropriate nurturing. [3]

Attachment itself does not depend on the kind of care the parent gives, but the quality of the attachment — whether it is secure or insecure — does. Infants become securely attached to a mother, father or other reliable caregiver who responds to their cries and meets their needs for comfort. Babies learn to trust that someone will soothe them and respond to them. This caregiver should be emotionally available and involved, aware of the baby's moods and needs, and able to respond appropriately.

To have secure attachment this primary relationship must start in early life, preferably within the first year, be reasonably consistent and stable over time and involve a reasonable portion of the child's daily activities.

Attachment is formed during that crucial time in an infant's development when the brain and nervous system are especially vulnerable to chronic stress and receptive to positive stimulation. Children who have the emotional security created by the experience of sensitive and responsive early nurturing will be more likely to have strong and enduring personal relationships with others later in life.

Babies' emotional development seems to be related to reinforcement or validation of emotions by their primary caregivers. If a parent shows delight at a new toy, baby will likely smile too. But a baby who is enjoying a toy may stop if the cues from the parent are negative. If a child is fearful in a new situation, and a parent is soothing and encouraging, the child will be more likely to explore than if the parent is non-committal or shows anxiety. Secure attachment provides a base from which a young child can venture forth.

With that emotional security created in the first year of life and maintained in early childhood, a young child is more likely to be able to face the world and other people with interest and confidence. Secure attachment to at least one parent has been shown to foster the development of self-confident, sociable and competent toddlers, preschoolers and school-age children.

Some babies are more difficult to look after than others. Some new parents sail relatively peacefully through the first year, while others are worn to a frazzle. Studies of the parent-child relationship have shown that even babies who are difficult — who may be colicky and cry all the time or grumpy and easily upset — can become securely attached if their parents learn to "read" their needs and respond to them. "This is not an intuition that a parent has or doesn't have," says Freda Martin, executive director of the Hincks Centre for Children and Adolescents in Toronto. "It's a skill that can be learned." ❹

DEVELOPMENT OF "TEMPERAMENT" AND ITS EFFECTS ON ATTACHMENT

The term "temperament" is generally considered to be a collection of individual characteristics that have a genetic predisposition evident at birth. It is shaped both by experiences and shapes experiences. Temperament is an individual's characteristic style of behaving in and responding to the world. Differences in temperament appear soon after birth. Babies respond differently to stimulation. Some are extremely active physically. Others are much less so. Some babies fuss and fret while others seem more content and tranquil.

Because temperament emerges soon after birth, it clearly has a strong genetic component. However, it's possible that very early experiences, including prenatal experiences, may also be a factor. ❺ A child's maturing temperament, in turn, affects many other developmental outcomes, such as getting along with others, coping with stress, meeting challenges and adapting to change.

If it is secure, the early attachment relationship promotes exploration and learning, as well as emotional stability. Freda Martin, child psychiatrist and executive director of the Hincks Centre for Children and Adolescents in Toronto, describes some of the longer-term consequences. "Secure attachment is critical to the development of coping skills and the ability to work cooperatively with other people. Many of the problems we have in our adult world come from people who cannot work well with others. It often goes back to attachment problems." **E1**

For instance, a cheerful, outgoing baby is more likely to get positive responses from adults than a baby who is cranky or withdrawn. In that way, a child influences his or her own environment. But a caregiver who provides consistent care, warmth and protection may prevent the anxious baby from turning into a fearful child. Or a fearful child may learn to overcome or control the tendency to withdraw from others. **5**

According to Paul Steinhauer, a child psychiatrist at The Hospital for Sick Children in Toronto, "an infant's temperament can interfere with the attachment relationship. When a poor fit occurs between the child's basic temperament and the needs of the parents, it can undermine the bonding process needed to build competence and resilience. But an easy-going temperament can buffer the child's reaction to stress and increase the child's adaptability and successful attachment." **6**

A growing child's temperament is influenced by the people around him or her. Just as important, the child's temperament affects the adults, who in turn further affect the child. This dynamic between the child's emerging temperament and his or her social environment continues from earliest infancy through adolescence.

The National Longitudinal Survey of Children and Youth (NLSCY) is the first large-scale Canadian study to include data on how babies' temperaments affect outcomes in later childhood. Early data showed that a parent's report of a baby's difficult temperament was often linked to families whose members were experiencing difficulties in resolving problems and relating to each other, to parents who were hostile to the baby, and to families in which the mother was young or experiencing postpartum depression. The survey's findings do not answer the question about the causes of difficult infant temperament, but they do suggest that the skills and abilities of the parents can make a difference. **7**

FEELING FOR OTHERS

Babies are social creatures and develop intense bonds with those who care for them. These early social interactions form the basis for later social relationships and emotional health in humans and other non-human primates. In fact, new evidence suggests that these early patterns of relating are also tied with early neural development by sculpting the neural pathways that result in young children learning new knowledge and understanding. **8**

An example is moral development — learning to understand what's right and wrong. Until relatively recently, it was believed that moral development started around age 4 to 6. Very young children were believed to make judgments simply based on what their parents told them to do or to avoid punishment. It was thought they didn't have their own conscience. **9**

Recent research, however, indicates that the beginnings of morality may start as young as a year and a half. Current studies concentrate on how children learn the rules of good behaviour such as taking turns and sharing toys, and develop an understanding of the feelings of others. **10**

Sensitivity to the distress of another may be a universal response built into all human beings, and the particular set of values that a child acquires depends on experience as the child develops — intellectually and emotionally. Adults guide the child's journey through this developmental process by giving guidelines, acting as models and talking about feelings.

Sometime during the second and third years, perhaps as young as 18 months, children begin to understand and show concern for actions that cause harm, such as a broken toy. They also begin to react to the distress of another child, and sometimes try to give comfort. Even before the age of four, children have been found to distinguish between social conventions, such as rules for lining up at daycare or dinner etiquette at home, and moral transgressions that are unfair or harmful to others. **10**

"'Moral intelligence' isn't acquired only by memorization of rules and regulations, by dint of abstract classroom discussion or kitchen compliance. We grow morally as a consequence of learning how to be with others, how to behave in this world, a learning prompted by taking to heart what we have seen and heard. The child is a witness; the child is an ever-attentive witness of grown-up morality — or lack thereof; the child looks and looks for cues as to how one ought to behave, and finds them galore as we parents and teachers go about our lives, making choices, addressing people, showing in action our rock-bottom assumptions, desires, and values, and thereby telling those young observers much more than we may realize." **E2**

Robert Coles

HELPING CHILDREN LEARN TO GET ALONG

Fear and anxiety about violence in our communities are growing. The studies of University of Montreal professor Richard Tremblay indicate that taking early steps to improve the social skills of aggressive and disruptive children may help reduce delinquency in adolescence. Delinquency in the teen years, in turn, is linked to adult criminal behaviour.

Tremblay headed up a two-year prevention program in Montreal that provided home-based parent training and school-based social skills training for disruptive kindergarten boys. The boys were identified as disruptive in kindergarten, but the social skills training and parent education intervention did not begin until boys entered Grade 2 — approximately 7 years old — and lasted until they were 9 years old. ⑪

Here's how the program worked. Families were visited once every three weeks for parent training sessions. These sessions included a reading program and training to monitor the child's behaviour, reinforce positive behaviour, punish effectively without being abusive, manage family crises and apply what they had learned. Social skills training for the boys included learning how to share and develop self-control. Follow-up included measuring behaviour, achievement at school and overall adjustment.

In adolescence, a significant difference was still evident between the aggressive boys who participated in the program and those who did not. At age 12, there were twice as many boys (44 percent) with serious adjustment difficulties at school in the non-treatment group as there were in the treatment group (22 percent). In addition, those in the program were more likely to be in the right school grade for their age, they were less prone to aggressive behaviour and their overall ability to adjust to school was rated as higher.

The boys in the program were also less likely to be involved in petty crimes such as trespassing or stealing bicycles and other property. For example, around 20 percent of the untreated boys, but only 5 to 7 percent of the treatment group, admitted having stolen bicycles and other property worth more than $10.

"There is a chance that our intervention succeeded in breaking the path between childhood disruptive behaviour and juvenile delinquency," says Tremblay. "Aggressive anti-social behaviour seems to crystallize by or around age 8. Our intervention around age 7 to 9 may have hit a sensitive period in these children's social development. The results may be even more effective, however, if we intervene at an earlier age." ⑫

Tremblay has reviewed the literature on 49 different prevention experiments working with preschool and school-age children to reduce risk factors that are believed to contribute to later delinquency and criminal behaviour. He concluded that the following factors in early childhood are associated with later delinquent behaviour:

LEARNING NOT TO HIT

The Collaborative Student Mediation Project is a program designed to reduce playground violence. The results are impressive — studies show that 90 percent of the conflicts were successfully resolved. Observations revealed at least an average of 50 percent reduction in playground physical violence. The project, which includes research studies, is a partnership between the Centre for Studies of Children at Risk, Chedoke Child and Family Centre, McMaster University and local boards of education. **B3**

The program, which relies on students as mediators, is also cost-effective. Student mediators participate in a 15-hour training program in conflict resolutions strategies. Mediator teams are on the playground during recess and lunch breaks at kindergarten and elementary schools. Mediators interrupt emerging conflicts, introduce themselves and ask children involved in the dispute whether they are ready to solve the problem. If students agree to the rules of the mediation process — each party must listen without interrupting, keep their hands and feet to themselves, and take responsibility for a solution — the mediator finds a quiet spot on the playground. Each child tells his or her side of the story and the mediator summarizes each position. Mediators encourage the children involved to explore potential solutions, agree on a plan and consider the prevention of future conflicts. Playground supervisors deal with students who refuse to participate or engage in more serious behaviours.

The program assists children who have difficulty getting along with others but who don't have access to professional help. It prevents minor disputes from escalating. Skills acquired in a more clinical type of treatment do not necessarily apply to the day-to-day world of the school playground. Student mediation seems to shift the prevailing views which regulate bullying and teasing within a school environment, by providing a consistent response to children who frequently get into fights and disputes with others.

~ childhood disruptive behaviour and intellectual deficits;

~ family characteristics, including parental discord, rejection of the child, ineffective discipline and poor supervision;

~ community characteristics, including a neighbourhood with high crime rates and disorganized schools; and

~ association with anti-social peers.

Some of the prevention programs he reviewed aimed at preventing delays in mental development among infants and toddlers through early childhood education and parent training. The programs focused on families and school-based activities. Tremblay recommends that prevention programs start before adolescence when problems tend to become more obvious and more severe. Prevention programs should continue for more than a year and tackle a range of child, family and community risk factors together. **13**

"Overall, early prevention programs help," says Tremblay. "Many of these studies were small. What impact could we have from larger-scale efforts? The indication from what we have learned so far is that we could substantially reduce the personal, social and economic costs of criminal behaviour in our society." **12**

LEARNING HOW TO PARENT

Being a good parent requires some skills that have to be learned. Successful parenting provides protection, promotes emotional stability and encourages exploration and learning.

Most parents get the skills they need from their own parents during their childhood. Parents remember what their parents did, and repeat that with their own children. Most people have generally positive experiences growing up. Even most parents who were neglected or abused in their own childhood have the abilities to be effective parents. But not all do. Nevertheless, all parents can benefit from learning and practising effective parenting skills.

There are two essential components of effective parenting skills: responsiveness and discipline.

THE FATHERS OF POINTE-CALUMET (E4)

A unique project called Prospère, in the Quebec community of Pointe-Calumet, is aimed at involving fathers more in the lives of their preschool children. The goal of Prospère is to encourage and maintain the commitment of fathers. The Pointe-Calumet project is an initiative of GRAVE (le Groupe de recherche et d'action sur la victimization des enfants/Research and Action Group on Child Abuse). One of the four priorities of GRAVE is promoting the involvement of fathers in family life and child raising.

One of the things project organizers noticed when they started looking into the "image" of fatherhood was that there wasn't one. In government offices, health institutions, social service agencies, in publications of all sorts, the image was nearly always of mother and child. A father was pictured occasionally, but mostly his role was ignored. That's something they're trying to change in Pointe-Calumet, a community of about 4,500 people northwest of Montreal.

It is now common for both parents to work outside the home. Many couples are sharing child-rearing responsibilities to a greater extent, although mothers usually carry the heaviest load. The involvement of fathers in parenting needs to receive greater attention and community support.

According to the 1991 report *Quebec: Crazy About Our Kids,* (E5) which was prepared for the province's health and social services ministry, too many fathers are absentee parents. Every child needs attentive and loving adults who are crazy about him or her. The report states that parents share the primary responsibility to make their children feel important, give them confidence in themselves and teach them they can count on others. But it also observed that responsibility doesn't stop with mothers, regardless of whether they work inside or outside the home.

Pointe-Calumet was chosen by GRAVE because it has a number of social problems, including a relatively high percentage of low-income families, single parents with children under 6 and parents with less than nine years of schooling. Some families were receiving social assistance.

Through activities and research, project organizers set out to define the specific needs of fathers. This included finding out how to meet men on their own ground — in their workplace and recreational settings — and to make access to community services more inviting. Prospère is working on initiatives such as trying to improve the accessibility of community services and educational activities so that more fathers will participate. To that end, it is providing flexible hours, extending invitations to fathers and organizing activities to improve parenting skills.

The project is also intended to change attitudes and expectations among fathers, mothers, service providers and the community so that they all place more value on fathers' contributions to the lives of their young children.

"You read these articles about these great men…whom you are supposed to admire, and they are notable because they worked all their lives for 20 years, 16 hours a day, and I just wonder what happened to their children all that time?"

A participant in the Fathers of Pointe-Calumet Program

Responsiveness includes providing warmth and expressing positive feelings; encouraging extensive verbal give-and-take in regular conversations between parents and children; involvement and interest in what the child is doing and saying; and sensitivity to what a child needs.

Appropriate discipline is firm but not excessively restrictive, and does not involve bullying or shaming. There are clear limits and expectations on children's actions; children are encouraged to take responsibility for their actions and to learn from the consequences of their behaviour. When confrontation becomes necessary, parents should encourage children to find acceptable alternatives to actions which are not acceptable.

According to Steinhauer, "These variables are interrelated, and are constantly working to reinforce and/or oppose each other. The parenting style that combines a high level of caring and involvement with high but reasonable expectations is most likely to help children develop the confidence, the competence, the coping skills needed to maintain competence and the sense of perspective that shapes how they react to stress. The interaction of these factors contributes to the achievement of resiliency." [14]

Data from the National Longitudinal Survey of Children and Youth showed that positive parenting practices, which included positive interactions and consistent supervision, help children get along with others. Positive parenting practices make a real difference, especially in families where there are challenges and difficulties for children. According to researchers Sarah Landy and Kwok Kam Tam of the Growing Together Project sponsored by the Hincks Centre for Children and Adolescents and the City of Toronto's Public Health Department, "Children in at-risk situations who enjoyed positive parenting practices achieved scores within the average range for children in Canada. Sometimes their outcomes even surpassed those of children who were living in more favourable sociodemographic conditions but who were exposed to less positive parenting practices or to more hostile/ineffective parenting." [15]

SUPPORTS FOR PARENTING

The teaching of parenting skills has been proven to be useful for parents from all socioeconomic groups. Research shows that overly harsh and restrictive parenting is harmful, and so is overly permissive parenting that provides no clear limits to behaviour. A balance of caring and discipline is needed, and this balance can be taught. **16**

Some adults who had a negative childhood and were taught that the way to resolve disputes or deal with anger is to hit someone will repeat the pattern, although most will not. But parents who were deprived of good parenting are less likely to know what good parenting is and how to do it.

Learning parenting skills is no panacea. Much of the damage done to children and young people in Canada is related to poor living conditions and lack of opportunities experienced by the children and their parents, circumstances that contribute to alienation and despair. Learning good parenting, however, can make a huge difference.

Aboriginal communities are dealing with the family and cultural dislocation caused when children were taken away from their Northern homes and put into residential schools. Those children, now adults, grew up in institutions instead of families — institutions that often neither understood nor appreciated their languages and cultures. As children, they were deprived of good parenting models. Programs like Skookum Jim in Whitehorse (described in the previous chapter) are trying to rekindle traditional values to support parents and parenting.

Given the wealth of information available on the importance of good parenting to positive child outcomes, and given the fact that parenting skills can be learned, supports for parenting should be part of an overall community-focused strategy. Such a strategy could include:

~ teaching skills to future parents in the schools;
~ parent support groups in community centres and schools;
~ public forums on challenging parenting issues like discipline; and
~ a network of coordinated community resources for parents.

As with early childhood education for preschoolers, support for parenting is likely to pay substantial social and economic dividends for society.

BABIES BEST START PROGRAM:

HELPING PARENTS AND CHILDREN — RIGHT FROM THE START

Babies Best Start is an early intervention program for low-income parents of children from birth to six years. **E6** Its primary objective is to promote optimal growth and development of parents and their infants and preschool children. The program recruits, trains and supervises parents from the community who are paid to provide a friendly home-visiting service to new parents of similar ethnocultural background. Parents are also encouraged to attend two group programs: Nobody's Perfect, which is a parent education course, and Mother Goose, which uses nursery rhymes and family games to help parents communicate and play with their children. The parent home visitors build a link between new parents who are often isolated and alone in the larger community.

An interim evaluation report found encouraging results. Parents report less stress and more pleasure in caring for their young children. There were positive changes in the home environments and improvements in children's general development. Further evaluation research is currently under way.

Babies Best Start was initiated by Metro Toronto Children's Aid Society in 1990 and is now funded by the federal government through the Community Action Program for Children and sponsored by Discoveries Child and Family Centre. It is based on the Hawaii Healthy Start Program designed to promote positive parenting, improve child health and development, prevent child neglect and abuse, and encourage better use of existing community resources. The Hawaii program has shown dramatic results in reducing child abuse and neglect among high-risk families. **E7**

To discover why some children blossom while others fail to thrive, researchers have analysed the NLSCY data and identified some of the parental circumstances that seem to make life more of a challenge for children. Some of the risk factors are parents with low levels of income, education or social support; single or teenage parents; parents with four or more children; and dysfunctional or depressed parents. Parents in any of these circumstances will be cheered to know that the effect of any one of these circumstances is usually small; a single risk factor does not doom a child to failure. Only those children exposed to four or more risk factors scored significantly lower in terms of their relationships, helping behaviour and their vocabulary. It's the cumulative effect of multiple risk factors that makes a child especially vulnerable. **E8**

SUPPORTING PARENTS IN OUR CHANGING SOCIAL AND ECONOMIC ENVIRONMENT

The rise in Canada's divorce rate

"The vast majority of Canadians marry at least once, and the majority of Canadian marriages do, for better or worse, last a lifetime. However, projections suggest that up to 40 percent of marriages entered into today will end in divorce." **17**

One major change in family relationships has been the rise in the divorce rate. The new Canadian reality is a broad range of family structures, including many blended families (remarried couples, sometimes each with children from a previous union) and a rising proportion of families (17 percent) with lone parents. **18** Communities have to respond to this change in the make-up of families.

Parental separation and divorce is hard on children, but it doesn't have to be crippling. The structure of the family is not what counts most. What counts for children is the warmth and stability of relationships within the family, however it is constituted. Children who know that both parents love them and are actively involved in their lives are more likely to come out of divorce situations feeling good about themselves and about family life. [19]

The break-up of families is especially hard on children if the result is drastically worsened living conditions. Single mothers are especially likely to have low incomes, which exposes their children to the stresses associated with poverty. These higher-risk children can benefit enormously from early childhood education, which supplements learning experiences at home.

Work and Family Stresses

Parents, particularly mothers, report that the combined demands of work and family are highly stressful. That stress affects both home and work life. At home, stress contributes to illness, affects the quality of parenting and creates marital conflict. At work, performance is affected if parents are distracted because the child care arrangements fell through or their child is ill, or they may be absent or late for work for those reasons. [20]

Family-friendly policies at work can alleviate family stress, especially in the early years of childhood. Such policies can take some of the pressure off juggling work and family responsibilities and contribute to more satisfying home life and better productivity at work. Unfortunately, many parents do not have the option of workplace child care, part-time work, flexible hours, job sharing, sick-child leave or extended maternity or family leave to take care of young children. [21]

Between 1981 and 1991, mothers with children at home accounted for most of the rise in the number of women in the workforce. In 1991, approximately two thirds of mothers who had children under age 6 were in the labour force. Ten years before, the comparative figure was only one half. [E9]

SOME FACTS ABOUT CHILD CARE (E10)

Many Canadian children are in child care.

▲ 1.5 million children, or 31 percent of children under age 12, are in regular non-parental child care (based on 1994 data).

The majority of these children are in unregulated and unlicensed child care.

▲ 27 percent of children in child care (about one in four children in child care) are in regulated child care programs. The other children (about three out of four) are in unregulated/informal arrangements such as relative care and in-home care.

High quality child care has the potential to benefit children's development while poor quality child care can harm their development.

▲ Research conducted in Canada and internationally demonstrates that when child care providers are responsive and warm, have some understanding of child development and are not responsible for too many children, child care can be just as beneficial, or more beneficial, than parent care — particularly in social and language skill development.

▲ Conversely, when caregivers are neglectful or harsh, unable to give individualized attention because they are responsible for too many children and there is inadequate stimulation, research shows that non-parental care can be harmful to children.

Research is demonstrating the advantages of regulated and licensed child care.

▲ Canadian and American research studies show that regulated care tends to be of higher quality than care that is unregulated or unlicensed.

Investments in providing high quality child care pay off in the short and long term.

▲ Children who enter Grade 1 with lower levels of social, language or thinking skills are more likely to experience problems in school, and more likely to drop out before high school graduation.

QUALITY CHILD CARE: AN INVESTMENT IN RELATIONSHIPS

Quality child care provides a positive and stimulating early childhood experience; it is a vital support for parents.

Quality child care builds relationships that nurture and stimulate development. Research shows that quality child care helps children develop well, while poor child care can harm development. Quality requires responsive adult caregivers. Just sitting a child down in front of a television set for hours, or providing a pile of toys, will not give the child the developmental stimulation needed in the preschool years. The adult caregiver must be involved with the child, and give the personal, individualized attention that is appropriate for the child's development. The caregiver must know the child well enough to respond appropriately as the child explores and reacts to the world around. **22**

OTHER CARING ADULTS CAN MAKE A MAJOR DIFFERENCE IN A CHILD'S LIFE

For many years, the study of adult-child relationships focused on the way that parents and their children bond. More recently, however, there has been greater recognition of the role that other people play in a child's development. Even just one significant other adult can make a world of difference. **23**

People who have overcome difficult family situations often point to one person who nurtured them at a crucial time in their development. It may have been an adoring grandparent, an understanding teacher, an inspiring coach or a thoughtful mentor.

Mary Ainsworth, a major figure in attachment theory, has noted that where a child's relationship with parents was insecure, "a secure relationship with some other important figure — a grandparent, a teacher, a coach, someone who was close and understanding — … functioned to make up for the life of insecurity with the parents." **24**

According to Ainsworth, a good relationship with a kindergarten teacher can be a developmental buffer for children considered at high risk for school failure. High-risk children did better in Grades 1 and 2 if they had developed a positive relationship with a kindergarten teacher. On the other hand, low-risk children who had a conflict-ridden or overly dependent relationship with the kindergarten teacher did worse than expected in Grades 1 and 2. **25**

Social supports — relationships with loved ones, friends and colleagues — are widely believed to influence the health of adults. The same is true, only more so, for young people growing up.

CONCLUSION

The most basic relationship in society is usually seen as mother and child. Mothers and fathers, however, need support from their own families and the broader community to develop healthy relationships with their children. And everyone in the community can play a role developing relationships with children. Some, like teachers and child care workers, do it as part of their work. Volunteers do it for free. Everyone who comes into contact with a child can help him or her on the road to healthy development, by protecting them from harm or even just by providing a smile or a word of encouragement.

ENDNOTES

1. Vygotsky, 1934, in Berk, 1994
2. Werner & Smith, 1992; Ainsworth & Marvin, 1995
3. Discussion on attachment based on Ainsworth & Marvin, 1995; Ainslie & Anderson, 1984 in Elicker & Fortner-Wood, 1995; Beckwith, 1990; Erikson, Stroufe & Egeland, 1985.
4. Martin, interview
5. Kagan, 1994
6. Steinhauer, interview
7. Normand et al, 1996
8. Keating, 1993
9. Kohlberg, 1969
10. Kuebli, 1994; Berk, 1997
11. Tremblay et al, 1994
12. Tremblay, interview
13. Tremblay & Craig, 1995

14. Steinhauer, interview
15. Landy & Tam, 1996, p. 109
16. Beckwith, 1990
17. Vanier Institute of the Family, 1994, p. 8
18. Canadian Council on Social Development, 1996
19. Garbarino, 1995
20. Higgins et al, 1993; Duxbury & Higgins, 1994
21. Beland, 1996
22. Doherty, 1996
23. Elicker & Fortner-Wood, 1995; Werner, 1996
24. Ainsworth & Marvin, 1995, p. 19
25. Elicker & Fortner-Wood, 1995

EXHIBIT ENDNOTES

E1. Martin, interview
E2. Coles, 1997, p. 5
E3. Cunningham et al, 1997
E4. Pointe-Calumet, 1995
E5. Quebec Ministry of Health and Social Services, 1991
E6. Andres et al, 1996
E7. Steinhauer, 1997
E8. Vanier Institute of the Family, 1997
E9. Logan & Belliveau, 1995
E10. Ross, Scott & Kelly, 1996; Doherty, 1996

Chapter 8
OPPORTUNITY AND HOPE:
The Third Determinant of Optimal Child Development

"I have been one of the lucky ones. I had supportive parents, good teach-ers and wonderful opportunities that I could take hold of…and did. But I also know that not everyone is that lucky and that I would not be who I am today if it were not for all the support and nurturance I received in my life. I also know the difference between how good it feels to have my opinion mean something and how small I feel when no one cares about what I have to offer.

There are many of us who have faced so many more challenges than our peers and yet have risen in the face of adversity. It is one thing to be a successful young person when you have a supportive environment and opportunities to learn and grow. It is another when there are not options or support systems available to you. Youth at risk who have overcome the odds, the stereotypes and the lack of sup-port — and have succeeded in attaining their goals — have the type of determina-tion and drive that gives me my inspiration.

If I were to define what it means for me to be healthy, I would have to answer — that besides food, shelter and clothing, a young person is truly healthy when listened to, given opportunities to grow and make their own mistakes, and loved for who they truly are and not for who someone wants them to be. I remem-ber someone once telling me that to be a healthy young individual, one basically needs to be competent and confident. Health is attaining one's own definition of success." **E1**

Zenia Wadhwani, Young Canadian Leader

T here is compelling new research that sheds light on the importance of factors that have often been neglected in investigations of child development: the factors of opportunity and hope. It is now clear that these are key determinants of optimal child development.

Opportunities are vital to healthy development because they can open up new pathways for children and young people. Risks to children's development can come not only from direct threats to health and well-being, but also from an absence of the opportunies that other children and youth have in our society.

All children need opportunities to grow and become part of society. It's all about a sense of hope. Younger children need chances to grow, play, explore and learn. Older children need to develop knowledge and skills, and to explore what interests them: What do I want to be? What am I good at? Adolescents need opportunities to be heard, to participate in the community, to learn about the real world, to practise responsible decision making. They need opportunities to work and to develop careers, so that they can find satisfying roles in society. Young people may also need a second chance, to go back and try again to get the skills and experience they may have missed. Chances to grow and learn throughout childhood and adolescence can make the difference between a person whose potential is realized and one whose potential is wasted.

HOPE AND ASPIRATIONS

Many opportunities could be available to children — from good schools to sports teams, art classes, community volunteering and cultural exchanges. What's important for children is having lots of different kinds of opportunities. These help create skills and the quality of resilience in children and young people. Opportunities motivate children and young people and help them achieve. Opportunities enable children and young people to build self-esteem and gain confidence. Opportunities lead to hope and aspirations for the future.

Youngsters who have a variety of opportunities in their lives are more likely to have an optimistic view of themselves as capable human beings. They seek out more positive opportunities because they have the confidence and the expectation that they can meet challenges.

Opportunities for young children lead to opportunities for teenagers and, in turn, good options for adults. The right opportunity at the right time can change a young person's life.

OPPORTUNITIES BUILD MOTIVATION AND EXPECTATIONS

Research into early educational experiences has found that their most lasting impact appears to be in the area of stimulating children's academic and career aspirations, their motivation and their commitment to learning. ❶

In the United States, Head Start is a program that has provided preschool for 3- to 5-year-olds from low-income families since the 1960s. Evaluations of the program show the children involved in Head Start made greater social and intellectual gains than children who weren't in the program. ❷ Head Start was designed to increase children's overall social skills, as well as academic achievement. The program also develops physical health, self-esteem and a sense of personal mastery or efficacy. Edward Zigler, who helped design Head Start, argues that being motivated can contribute more to a person's success in school, work and society than intelligence. ❸

There is enough accumulated evidence to show that Head Start has helped children's adjustment to school, their health, their family lives and social skills, at least during the primary school years. Teachers tend to see them as more competent in school, and their families tend to be more involved in their children's education and have higher expectations of schooling. ❸

Other studies of early education programs have made similar findings. Children who attend quality preschool programs, particularly disadvantaged children, tend to do better in school. They are less likely to be held back a grade or be put in a special class. An important ingredient in this school success is motivation. It seems that early educational experiences help to change the "achievement orientation" of the child and family. Children in these studies were more likely to give achievement-related answers if asked to talk about something they had done that made them feel proud. Mothers of children in preschool programs had higher hopes and expectations for their children. ❹

The High/Scope Project is often cited as proof of long-term benefits of high quality, intensive early education for disadvantaged children. It was a demonstration project in the 1960s of the High/Scope Educational Research

Foundation in Ypsilanti, Michigan. About 60 "graduates" of the Perry Preschool (see also Chapter 2) have been tracked over the past quarter-century, and compared with a group of similar children who were not in the preschool program (the control group). At age 27, the Perry graduates did significantly better than their control group peers in terms of high school completion, employment and earnings, and avoidance of criminal arrest and use of social services. **5**

Researchers looking for an explanation of these improved outcomes point to factors such as attitudes to school and commitment to learning fostered in the preschool years. Dan Offord, director of the Centre for Studies of Children at Risk in Hamilton, Ontario notes that "this research illustrates how the program put kids on a pathway that was less harmful, and empowered the parents to be advocates for their kids. Providing children with new opportunities over time — opportunities they would otherwise not receive — can put kids on a better pathway." **6**

Student motivation to learn and parental expectations of schooling also show up in other studies. A well-known review of the effects of education on children's development by Michael Rutter of Britain concluded that "the long-term educational benefits stem not from what children are specifically taught, but from effects on children's attitudes to learning, on their self-esteem, and on their task orientation." He also noted that "learning how to learn may be as important as the specifics of what is learned." **7**

The Quality of a School Matters

A child's "readiness to learn" when entering school is strongly tied to family background (especially income) and preschool experiences. But once a child enters school, the quality of that environment also makes a difference to learning, according to research in Canada and other countries. Differences in schools contribute to differences in academic achievement, even after taking into account family background and children's abilities upon entering school.

Children's access to preschool educational opportunities varies across Canada. All 6-year-old children, however, must attend a school setting

SCIENCE AND GIRLS E2

Women may have broken through all kinds of employment barriers in the last two or three decades, but young girls are still very susceptible to societal messages about what a girl should be like. If the message little girls hear is that they are not supposed to be good at science and math, they may comply, since compliance tends to be rewarded in girls (boys are more likely to be rewarded for assertiveness).

Les Scientifines is a Montreal program that provides an after-school "club" for girls aged 9 to 12. The club features science-based activities to counter stereotypes and help girls succeed at school. A high percentage of the participants are from lone-parent homes and almost half are from diverse ethnic backgrounds. Les Scientifines' main goals are to counter the negative effects of gender-role stereotyping, and to help girls gain new knowledge, develop positive work and living habits and prevent school failure.

There are activities four days a week for about 30 participants a day. To encourage girls to participate, two facilitators wait after school to accompany them to the project location. Activities are free of charge. The participating students receive support for their school projects and are helped to improve their ability to think, act and make decisions.

Les Scientifines truly is a community-based partnership. The neighbourhood social service organization provides technical support, offers snacks and provides professional services like counselling to the program's facilitators and student participants. The City of Montreal loans space to hold the program. The school board provides financial support. And the staff of the neighbourhood schools maintain close contact with the program.

The results? Regular participants have better problem-solving skills, improve their understanding of cause and effect relationships, develop curiosity about their physical environment, and learn patience and perseverance. The greater their participation, the stronger their motivation to excel at school.

or be in approved alternative home schooling. The vast majority of Canadian children attend public schools for 12 years — six hours a day, five days a week, 36 weeks of the year for a total of about 15,000 hours by high school graduation.

Public schools provide an equal opportunity to all students regardless of income level, family background, gender, religion, ethnicity or race. An important measure of schooling's success is literacy, broadly defined as "using printed and written information to function in society, to achieve one's goals and to develop one's knowledge and potential." **8** Levels of literacy skills provide a measure of how students are prepared to participate in the Canadian knowledge-based economy. Differences in literacy skills among students with differing family backgrounds and characteristics also indicate whether schools are providing students with equitable opportunities.

Successful schools provide educational opportunities which support literacy skills and other academic achievements for all children and youth. In the process, they reduce differences in outcomes and the overall achievement level of students rises. Successful schools are characterized by a number of common elements, including: **9**

~ higher levels of parental involvement;

~ higher teacher expectations of student achievement;

~ relevant curriculum content with emphasis on specific literacy skills;

~ collaboration among administrators, teachers and students;

~ positive school climate where students feel safe and have a sense of belonging;

~ high levels of participation in extracurricular activities;

~ integration of students from differing social class backgrounds and ability levels; and

~ an emphasis on prevention over remediation.

Douglas Willms of the Atlantic Centre for Policy Research in Education at the University of New Brunswick studies how schools affect children and youth and how social class differences relate to differences in education outcomes. According to Willms, "Research from a number of countries has provided convincing evidence that schools and schooling systems can vary considerably in their effects on children's outcomes, and that their effectiveness depends on their social context. Three of the most important features of school context concern the norms and expectations established by teachers and principals, the disciplinary climate of the school and the support of parents and the wider community." **10** If children from differing socioeconomic backgrounds have equal access to supportive school contexts (not just equal opportunity to get in the door), there are fewer differences in achievement outcomes such as literacy. The gap between children who come from "advantaged" family backgrounds and those from less advantaged backgrounds will be narrowed.

One of Willms's research studies looked at children's academic skills between Grades 3 and 7 at 31 elementary schools in British Columbia. Children attending one of the three best-performing schools gained more skills than those attending one of the four worst-performing schools. Even after taking into account children's family backgrounds, the reading scores of children in the best-performing schools were about six to eight months ahead of those in the worst-performing schools. Children from less advantaged home backgrounds attending the best-performing schools were likely to show more improvement in their reading skills than advantaged children who attended the worst-performing schools. **11**

Schools exert a big influence on learning and development — both cognitive and social — for 12 years. They can support children who arrive ready to learn and can remove barriers for children who need extra support to be successful. But school environments can also maintain the gaps in abilities that children bring to their first day in school.

The National Longitudinal Survey of Children and Youth informs us that in Canadian public schools, the ability gap is maintained. The poorest children were likely to be in remedial classes and least likely to be rated by their teachers as near the top of the classes in reading or mathematics. The children from the highest income families were most likely to be in gifted classes and least likely to be in remedial classes. **12**

Schools located in low-income communities often do not have the same access to resources and supports as those in more affluent neighbourhoods. Affluent parents can raise more money for computers and extracurricular activities. Some school boards allocate additional financial resources to schools in low-income areas, but it is often not enough to provide the same level of resources and support as those in high-income areas.

Schools have the potential to provide opportunity for all children. We need to organize and provide resources to schools to make sure that children have equal chances to participate in all activities and equal likelihood of academic success despite different starting points.

SELF-CONFIDENCE AND OPPORTUNITY

Self-confidence is not something that can be handed to children. It must be developed from within. It is often based on their experiences with the challenges they have managed to meet and on the supportive relationships they have with others.

Feeling capable of exercising control over one's actions and environment is known as self-efficacy. It is considered to be an important influence on development because such beliefs influence the level of a person's motivation, perseverance in the face of setbacks, the quality of analytical thinking, and vulnerability to stress and depression. [13]

Children who have a healthy degree of self-efficacy tend to look at difficult problems as something to be solved and as a way to learn more skills. Children who have low self-efficacy tend to see problems as an indication of their own low ability and a route to failure. They are more likely to feel helpless in the face of challenges. [14]

Most people are on a continuum between utmost confidence and abject helplessness. Studies of children's reaction to criticism of their play in kindergarten indicated that belief in oneself or lack of it is already detectable at a young age. This suggests it is important to start very early in helping to build up children's sense of what they can do and what they can aspire to.

Parents' feelings of self-efficacy — their belief in their own ability to support their children's development — make a difference. Parental support and parental expectations reinforce their children's belief in themselves and their abilities.

A child's positive beliefs and aspirations also contribute to achievement by fostering peer acceptance and reducing depression and problem behaviour. Young people who believe they can manage educational demands and maintain satisfying friendships are better able to withstand setbacks. [13]

HOPE AND ASPIRATIONS DEPEND ON OPPORTUNITY AND EQUITY

Risks to children's development can come not only from direct threats to health and well-being, but also from an absence of opportunities. Lack of opportunity can undermine self-esteem. It can destroy motivation and hope. Poor parents often have high expectations for themselves and their children. Nevertheless, it is more difficult to teach children that the world is full of opportunities if experience teaches them otherwise.

Carolyne Gorlick, of the University of Western Ontario in London, has done research with low-income single mothers and their children. In a study of families headed by single mothers who were leaving the welfare system, she found that these women lacked neither motivation nor expectations for themselves and their children. But they faced many obstacles, notably "the unequal playing field of education and employment in which they are required to take chances." [15]

The support and love these mothers gave their children made a real difference to their children's self-esteem. The more maternal support a child felt he or she received, the higher the child's perceptions of him or herself. There seemed to be a limit, however, to how much mothers could contribute to their children's feelings of self-worth. That limitation, Gorlick says, points to the need for other people in the child's life — like teachers, coaches, employers and friends — to provide support and opportunities.

Older children in the study expressed an understanding of the struggle their mothers were going through to keep the household going, and of the inequities in society. They looked at other families, and wondered why they had so little when others had so much. One 15-year-old girl said proudly, "No,

I don't feel poor. My mom puts me ahead of herself so I can get what I need."
A 16-year-old boy commented, "The name 'welfare' is a problem, because
when you hear it in school, welfare sounds like you have lost hope, and I
haven't." **16**

Hope is undermined when a society fails to demonstrate a commitment to equity and opportunity for all. All of Canada's children should have
an equal chance to live their dreams. They don't have equal abilities or talents, but they should have equal access to opportunities and equal participation in them.

Hope and aspirations stem from being able to see a place of worth
and standing for oneself — in the family, at school, at work, in the community. A young person who sees no opportunities ahead will have difficulty
imagining a better future. Discrimination in all its ugly forms undermines
opportunity, self-esteem and hope. An absence of role models for minority
and disadvantaged youth creates a vacuum in which it is difficult to forge
images that bolster self-esteem.

HOPE AND CHILD SURVIVAL: AN AMERICAN HYPOTHESIS

A remarkable study in the United States looked at why more
African-American babies die than white babies. The infant mortality rate
among American blacks is about double that of whites. Two thirds of babies
who die have low birth weight. In a paper given to the Child Health 2000
world congress in Vancouver in 1992, researchers Charles Lowe and
Margaret Boone said that after systematically accounting for all the major
risk factors, they were still left with an "unexplained residual" of 15 to 20
percent more infant deaths among African-Americans. **17**

This gap is related to poverty, but it is not caused by economic disadvantage alone. It is related to lack of social supports for pregnant women
from family and community, but it is not caused by that alone either. Many
of the poor African-American women studied did not receive adequate prenatal care, but lack of access to medical services was not enough to
account for the differential between white and African-American infant
mortality rates.

Lowe and Boone suggest that the unexplained residual is caused by hopelessness, lack of a sense of future, of meaning, of control over what happens to one's life. They argue that it is the responsibility of all people to enable all members of society to have a sense of hope. If people's feelings about their prospects in life improve, other changes, such as family and social supports, will follow. The most successful strategy to reduce infant death among poor urban blacks, they argue, is to bring young black men, particularly between the ages of 18 and 25, into the workforce so they can reconnect with their communities and support their families.

In Canada, we like to think we don't have the same problems as they do in the United States, and in some significant areas, we are right. We do not have the same levels of violence, particularly violence related to firearms; we do not have the same problems in our major inner cities with poverty and "ghettoization"; teenage pregnancies in the States are high, while the Canadian rate has been declining for some years; and we continue to maintain a publicly financed universal health care system.

On the other hand, there are a number of children growing up in grinding poverty in Canada. There are people living on the streets of all our major cities. Systemic racism and other forms of discrimination are still prevalent in our society. It may be useful, therefore, to see how studies such as those by Lowe and Boone may provide insights for us.

OPPORTUNITY AND DISCRIMINATION

An Ontario study that asked young school-aged children about their images of success found that both boys and girls in a racially mixed group defined success as a man with white skin wearing a suit and carrying a briefcase. [18] Another consultation project survey among young people identified racism as something that blocked them from communicating with each other and being themselves. [19]

Schools are often cited as places where children should be taught tolerance. But we make it harder for schools to be successful if children learn at home or in the community that it is acceptable to be intolerant. Children need to see demonstrated in their daily lives that people in their communities respect each other's heritages and celebrate diversity.

Young children, regardless of race, should see that there are opportunities for their parents in the employment market and in community leadership roles. Young people looking for their own places in the community need to see that there is a fair chance for them. A young person who sees life as a dead end may be in danger of fulfilling his or her own expectations.

We need only to look at the statistics on Aboriginal children to see how far we have to go to become a society that offers equal opportunities to all our children. The infant mortality rate among status Indian and Inuit babies is about double the national rate. Aboriginal children are more likely than other children to live in inadequate housing and to go hungry. Suicides by young Aboriginal people have devastated some Aboriginal communities. [20]

Madeleine Dion Stout of the Centre for Aboriginal Education, Research and Culture at Carleton University in Ottawa sees the will and resourcefulness of Aboriginal children as key to reclaiming their future. "Their stories can often be uplifting. Instead of dwelling so much on deficits, we must recognize children's tenacity and resiliency and build on them. Their survival spirit is strong." [21]

ROOTS OF TOLERANCE OR INTOLERANCE

As we live in a culturally, racially and linguistically diverse society, it is critical for children to become comfortable and accepting of people from various backgrounds. It is easier to develop tolerance during the early years, when children are first aware of physical differences and can learn to accept these differences as positive — rather than react to them with fear or anger.

Children as young as 2 and 3 years old are aware of physical differences such as skin colour or genitals. By 4 or 5 years of age, many children are developing set attitudes toward people who are from other racial or cultural groups, or from different family groupings. [22] Children also develop definite attitudes toward male and female roles and expectations that are, of course, affected by the biases of Canadian society.

Around the age of 4 or 5, children develop a concept of their own racial and cultural identity which contributes to their self-concept or definition of self. Children who experience racial, cultural or ethnic name calling or put-downs feel inferior about themselves. ㉒ This is also the time when children begin to learn that society values some people more than others. The preschool years, therefore, are the time to counteract prejudices and discrimination based on race, culture, gender, economic status and sexual orientation.

FAIR PLAY

All children want to participate in recreational activities with other children, whether these activities are as casual and unstructured as playing together on the sidewalk, or as formal and structured as playing in a school sports league.

Recreational opportunities do more than promote good physical development in children. They also give them a chance to relate to others, and a sense of achievement from mastering skills.

Once children get behind in their recreational skill development, they are less likely to pursue sports and arts programs at school because they can't keep up with their peers, they don't make the teams and their self-esteem suffers. A consequence of not participating in these types of orga-nized activities before and after school is that these children and adolescents have time on their hands — and some of them get into trouble.

Formal recreational programs tend to have fees and equipment costs that deter families with few resources. Just getting a child to an arena for hockey practice before school may be a problem for a low-income parent without a car. A spare $300 to $400 for football camp is simply out of reach for a low-income family. Even if a teenager can earn $400 at a part-time job over a period of time, there may be more pressing family needs for that extra money.

"It is difficult to think of another area in children's lives in Canada in which economically disadvantaged children are treated so unfairly," says Offord. ㉓

A 1977 study in Ottawa of children, aged 5 to 15, demonstrated that children from low-income homes don't have the same chances to develop

I would love to go to football camp, but I have never asked to because I know that my mother has a really hard time and these football camps cost $300 to $400. I did talk to my junior football coach once about going on a field trip, and the school spotted me the money and I did pay them back. I always pay back my debts. I don't know this time because it may be the senior coach who sends you to camp, and I don't know him as well. **13**

Mike, age 16

recreational skills in sports and arts programs as other children. Children from a subsidized housing project in Ottawa were significantly behind those from a middle-class neighbourhood in participation and achievement in recreational activities. **24**

Only 35 percent of children from the public housing units had ever played a musical instrument, while 77 percent of middle-class children had. Thirteen percent of the low-income group had played on a coached hockey team, compared with 29 percent of their better-off peers. The children from low-income homes who got into recreational activities tended to start them later, and to reach the high skill levels later, compared to middle-class children.

The Ontario Child Health Study carried out in the 1980s confirmed that economically disadvantaged children had far fewer opportunities to develop skills in sports and art. For example, 35 percent of the children growing up in families with a total family income of less than $10,000 had participated in coached sports, compared with 60 percent of children in families with higher incomes. There was also a large gap in participation in art classes. **25**

A free, recreational skill development program for low-income children aged 5 to 15 in Ottawa and Hamilton, Ontario began in the 1980s. These programs are still operating. Both cities have found that participation is high and children progress well through various skill levels. Public housing complexes where the program was offered saw a decline in vandalism, mischief and behavioural problems among the children. Children in the program made better use of their time, found healthy role models and improved their self-esteem as they learned new skills.

Offord was a principal investigator in the Ottawa and Hamilton program and still runs, after four decades, a summer recreational skill camp for economically disadvantaged children called Christie Lake Camp located outside Ottawa. **26**

NOURISH THE SPIRIT **27**

The famous child psychiatrist, Robert Coles, author of *The Spiritual Life of Children* and *The Moral Intelligence of Children*, writes of children "as seekers, as young pilgrims well aware that life is a finite journey and as anxious to make sense of it as those of us who are farther along in the time allotted us." **28** Children's search for the meaning of life is their most profound expression of self and a key aspect of their development as human beings.

One of the earliest signs of beginning to reach out to the spiritual and mysterious is children's passionate effort to understand the world around them — "Why is the sky blue? Why don't we have wings like birds?" We all share this lifelong quest. While our knowledge increases enormously, we always remain bounded by the horizon of the unknown. Life remains filled with "why?" — with the search for meaning.

Search for meaning often becomes poignant as the child faces the larger questions of life. A child asks, "Why does my friend get sick? Why are there poor people sleeping on the streets? Why do some children have so little and others so much?" They begin to address issues of justice and fairness and to sense the arbitrariness of inequity and suffering.

The experience of joy and wonder is also spiritual. The beauty of the butterfly, or the sparkle of the dew in the perfect pattern of a spider's web, or the sudden thrill of a bird's song teaches children that life is full of unpredictable magic. Nature and the environment are experienced more and more as part of a larger vision of concern that means a great deal to many young people. Music, too, can have a great impact on the spirit. Music not only teaches, it often helps children to gain a spiritual sense.

As with all else, it is first the family's culture that shapes the child's spiritual vision. Some families transmit to their children faith in a power, a providence that is on their side. Those beliefs can give courage and a sense of hope.

Spiritual vision gives children a buffer against life's darker moments, a sense of a firm place to stand. To achieve such spiritual vision, children need opportunities to experience art, nature, science and human connections. They need the time and peace to reflect on their experiences and observations of the world. They need to be taught reverence and respect for creativity and a sense of stewardship for living things. They should be encouraged to help others and to see the world through the eyes of those who are marginalized and discriminated against. To deprive children of the opportunity to nurture their innate spirituality is to diminish their lives.

LISTEN! E4

Young people want to have a say about the things they see as important. Too often, the adult world dismisses their point of view. Youth need many opportunities to voice their concerns, particularly on issues that affect their own well-being.

If you listen to Canadian children and young people, you can hear reflected — at times quite graphically — many of the pressures that weigh on families, on neighbourhoods and on our society.

An anecdotal survey of Ontario schoolchildren was conducted in 1993 by Insight Canada Research for the [then] Ontario Premier's Council on Health, Well-being and Social Justice. Called the Aspirations Report, it found that youngsters in Grades 1 and 2 were already aware of violence, abuse, family discord, poverty and pollution. These little ones talked about food being "too expensive for my mother," wanting "the fighting to stop in the apartment in front of us," yearning for more space at home "because there is no room to play" and wishing for a neighbourhood with "people who would be nicer." E5

Many older children and adolescents involved in the same survey displayed great anxiety about the world and their future. The group of 9- to 11-year-olds sketched a future of social and environmental breakdown: "lots of poor people in the street" — "the rainforest will be gone" — "there will be garbage everywhere" — "there will be lots of killing for no reason of animals and people" — "I'll be scared to go outside" — "there will be gangs and drugs."

The adolescents who were surveyed, while looking forward to independence, were anxious about their economic prospects. Many of these young people were critical of their schooling and how they were being prepared or not prepared for the real world. These teenagers also talked about the importance of relationships, about needing friends, parents and teachers who cared about them.

These young voices provide a candid snapshot of what some children of different ages and from different communities and backgrounds are thinking and feeling — in their own words. We should listen.

ENDNOTES

1. Sylva, 1992

2. Lee, Brooks-Gunn & Schnur, 1988 in Sylva, 1994

3. Zigler & Styfco, 1994

4. Lazar & Darlington, 1982 in Sylva, 1994

5. Schweinhart et al, 1993

6. Offord, interview

7. Rutter, 1985, p. 700 in Sylva, 1994, p. 142

8. OECD & Statistics Canada, 1995, p. 14 in Willms, 1996B, p. 5

9. King & Peart, 1990; Sylva, 1992, Willms, 1997

10. Willms, 1997 (in press), p. 23

11. Willms & Jacobsen, 1990 in Willms 1996B

12. Human Resources and Development Canada & Statistics Canada, 1997

13. Bandura et al, 1996

14. Dweck & Leggett, 1988 in Sylva, 1994

15. Gorlick, 1995, p. 73

16. Gorlick, 1995, p. 7-9

17. Lowe & Boone, 1992

18. Insight Canada Research, 1993

19. Ontario Coalition for Children and Youth, 1994

20. Canadian Institute of Child Health, 1994A

21. Stout, 1996, p. 23

22. Derman-Sparks & the A.B.C. Task Force, 1989

23. Offord, interview

24. Offord & Jones, 1991

25. Offord et al, 1987

26. Offord, interview

27. This section is adapted from an unpublished article by Dr. Colin Maloney, executive director of the Catholic Children's Aid of Metropolitan Toronto, 1996

28. Coles, 1990, p. xvi in Maloney, 1996, p. 1

EXHIBIT ENDNOTES

E1. Wadhwani, 1996, p. 2-3

E2. Carignan, 1992 & Chamberland, interview

E3. Gorlick, 1995, p. 9

E4. Insight Canada Research, 1993

E5. Excerpts from the Aspirations Report, Insight Canada Research, 1993

Chapter 9
COMMUNITY IS US:
The Fourth Determinant of Optimal Child Development

C hildren don't just grow up in families. They also grow up in social settings that range from child care centres and schools to brownie packs and sports teams. Human beings are social animals. They need other people. Communities used to be simple to understand when people lived in a village or a small neighbourhood. Today, the mobility of families, cars and telephones have changed the nature of communities. But communities exist everywhere in society. Children need their supportive environments. And communities depend on young people for their futures.

THE IMPORTANCE OF A CHILD'S SOCIAL ENVIRONMENT

James Garbarino is the director of the Family Life Development Centre and professor of Human Development and Family Studies at Cornell University in Ithaca, New York. His work has explored how various social environments in families, schools and neighbourhoods influence the development of growing children, with a particular focus on the effects of child abuse and violence.

Garbarino likens the development of children to drawing a map or, as he calls it, a "social map." The child's map evolves out of the relationship between the child and the child's world — how the world reacts to the child, and with time and experience, how the child reacts to the world. As children grow older, their connections and their immediate social and physical environments expand. "Life draws the child's map; each child sees the world through the lenses of culture, temperament, and individual experience," writes Garbarino. "The child proceeds with the drawing of this map in response to experiences that arise from the social systems of family, school, neighbourhood, church, community, society, and culture.

"Some children learn to draw maps in which they are central figures, powerful and surrounded by allies. Others draw defensive maps in which they are surrounded by enemies, or are insignificant specks stuck off in a corner. Does the child expect help when in need? Does the child fear strangers? Does the child trust other children? Does the child expect adults to cause pain? To give comfort? Does the child see a safe and secure place in the world? The social map holds the answer to these questions." **1**

The home, neighbourhood, school, community and government all have a role to play in shaping each child's future.

COMMUNITY IS EVERYWHERE

Families and their children work, play, learn and grow in communities. A country as big as Canada is made up of a mesh of different communities which range in size from a half dozen neighbours to congregations, schools, cities, provinces and even the entire country. Most people belong to many communities that overlap.

WELCOME

In North Bay, Ontario, out front of the newly built Sunset Park Public School, there is one of those big freestanding signs that usually advertise brake jobs or doughnut shops. Here the message shouts out: "Visitors Welcome. It Takes a Village to Raise a Child."

A community should be a place of belonging. If children and young people are to find positive role models to follow, if they are to get opportunities to learn responsibility and make healthy choices, if they are going to be able to envision a future full of possibilities — they are going to achieve these within a community. Community is not just government, although government is part of community. It is not just the local service club or volunteers who help others, although they are part of community, too. It is families, workplaces, schools, parks, police, libraries, media ... it is the sum of all our parts and how we live together.

A sense of community is also reflected in the societal institutions we share, such as our health care system, pension programs for the elderly, school systems for the young, supports for the unemployed and the poor. We tend to think of these institutions as belonging to the government, but government is only the fundraiser. These institutions are the embodiment of what we as Canadians have decided to do for and with each other.

A sense of community is a sense of the common good. It is what animates collaborative action. It is shared involvement and responsibility. Community becomes a determinant of healthy development when it works to provide quality environments for children and families.

Julie White, executive director of the Trillium Foundation in Ontario, underscores five capacities or characteristics of successful communities: an abundance of social capital; strong connections with the outside world; a willingness to welcome and integrate newcomers; the ability to innovate; and the capacity to collaborate. **E1**

COMMUNITY SPANS GENERATIONS AND FOSTERS PARTNERSHIPS

Community is vital as a sustaining environment for children and families. At its best, community provides a sense of belonging, and is an expression of common interests and shared involvement.

One of the strengths of community is that it spans generations and fosters partnerships. Children grow up and adults grow old together. Ideally, community provides a perspective on the whole generational spectrum — the baby born today will be the parent of the next generation 20 or 30 years from now. There is no us versus them. There is just us.

COMMUNITY AS SOCIAL CAPITAL

Harvard's Robert Putnam, an influential thinker on community, has spent over 20 years studying what is, for many, a rather obscure topic — the creation of new regional governments in Italy in the 1970s. His analysis of the Italian experience, however, has led him to some far-reaching conclusions for democracies and economies everywhere. **2**

In *Making Democracy Work* (1993), Putnam concluded that the reason the experiment in regional government worked so well in the North of Italy (and not well in the South) was because of long-standing local traditions of "civic community, that is, patterns of civic involvement and social solidarity." **3** The study also considered the relative prosperity of the North compared to the South. In Putnam's analysis, in addition to supporting effective democratic institutions, civic community is also a predictor of economic prosperity.

Putnam writes that, "civic traditions alone did not trigger (nor, in that sense 'cause') the North's rapid and sustained economic progress over the last century; that takeoff was occasioned by changes in the broader national, international and technological environment. On the other hand, civic traditions help explain why the North has been able to respond to the challenges and opportunities of the nineteenth and twentieth centuries so much more effectively than the South." **3**

Putnam traced the emergence of civic traditions in the North of Italy back to the beginning of the twelfth century. But he did not find that the basis for civic life resides in a lifestyle of the past. On the contrary, the vibrant modernism and urbanism of the northern cities have continued to support civic life, while the small towns and rural communities of the South have not done so to the same extent.

What makes up civic community? Putnam suggests the following:

— **Civic engagement:** Citizenship in a civic community is marked by active participation in public affairs, with an emphasis on shared rather than personal interest. "Citizens in a civic community, though not selfless saints, regard the public domain as more than a battleground for pursuing personal interest." **4**

— **Political equality:** There are equal rights and obligations for all. People are bound together by "horizontal relations of reciprocity and cooperation, not by vertical relations of authority and dependency." ❹

— **Solidarity, trust and tolerance:** Conflict and controversy will always be present, but solutions and compromises are more likely in an atmosphere of mutual trust.

— **Associations or social structures of cooperation:** Associations are participatory local organizations that are self-generated, not imposed or implanted from outside.

Putnam contrasts pro-community attitudes of enlightened self-interest with the "amoral familism" that supports protecting and promoting the short-term interests of one's own nuclear family.

> Readers who are interested in the topic of civic community may want to look at *Civil Society: Reclaiming Our Humanity* by Sherri Torjman of the Caledon Institute of Social Policy. ❷

CANADA'S SOCIAL CAPITAL

"Social capital" is a term that describes the mutual trust, cooperation and involvement in public affairs that flourish in a community. Investing in social capital provides a return, just as investing financial capital can yield a profit.

How large and solid is Canada's stock of social capital? Our ideal of "peace, order and good government" is at least partly an expression of our sense of community, but we have not yet fully built up our national reserves of social capital.

Equalization payments that come from richer provinces and are paid to poorer ones through the national tax system are an expression of solidarity and sharing. Our publicly supported health care system that provides medical care to all Canadians is another. So are the wide range of community-initiated projects aimed at supporting people in their daily lives.

Building up social capital enables people to meet new economic and social challenges and to solve their problems together. That, in turn, increases prosperity and promotes effective government.

If we deal with economic and fiscal problems by increasing inequality, we will undermine the trust and cooperation that contribute to social capital. If we fail to protect those least able to protect themselves — our children — we will undermine our collective future.

Judith Maxwell, who heads up the Canadian Policy Research Networks, believes that we are currently at a crossroads that offers two options: a polarized society and a resilient society.

The polarized society is characterized by marginalization of certain vulnerable groups like young people, minorities and low-skilled workers; less social spending and more spending on security; a widening gulf between highly skilled and well-paid professional and technical workers and poorly skilled, low-paid workers who are constantly threatened by unemployment; and the retreat of the middle class from civic responsibility.

The resilient society, as Maxwell describes it, is one in which "people develop ways to adapt to the new labour market and new family structures. They take responsibility for themselves and their colleagues, neighbours and kin. New forms of collective action emerge to strengthen communities. Public investments in human and social capital are given priority." **5**

The forces of polarization are strong. Communities are being destabilized by economic restructuring, and more people are becoming marginalized. But at the same time, research shows that Canadians identify strongly with the values of self-reliance, moral responsibility to help each other and investing in future generations. **6**

If the resilient society is to win out in the twenty-first century, says Maxwell, we must make those values the basis of public policy and private action. We must invent new forms of collective action.

VALUES, SOCIAL POLICY AND COMMUNITIES

Most people understand that parents who can find only marginal employment, are living in poor housing, have no experience in raising a child and have few supports from family or service agencies may be hard pressed to provide a healthy and hopeful nurturing environment for their child. Supports do make a difference.

The American experience, for example, shows a strong correlation between infant mortality, child maltreatment and poverty. A study of factors associated with child maltreatment in Omaha, Nebraska in 1978 found that the socioeconomic status of neighbourhoods accounted for 40 percent of the difference in maltreatment rates across neighbourhoods. However, a later replication of the study in Montreal found a much weaker association between socioeconomic status and child maltreatment rates. Researchers presume that, because the welfare policies in Montreal were more generous and families had access to more support services, families' socioeconomic status had less of an impact on child maltreatment rates. **7**

Knowing this, the community — and society as a whole — has a choice: whether or not to alleviate the effects of poverty by ensuring that all families receive the supports they need.

These days, some Canadians see our social policies as much more interventionist than those in other countries, but that is in comparison to the Americans. Compared to Japan and many European countries, Canada is positively hands-off when it comes to supporting children and families. Canada has to chart its own course. Canadians are generally more willing than Americans to see governments play a role in society, especially when it comes to providing social programs for children. In fact, that difference is often seen as a key part of the Canadian identity.

The *Exploring Canadian Values* report, published in 1995 by the Canadian Policy Research Networks, revealed that deeply held Canadian values concerning social objectives have not changed dramatically over time, **6** but there has been a revolution in the way Canadians want these values to be realized in social programs.

~ A majority of Canadians, seven in ten, see social programs as essential to Canadian identity.

~ Canadians are worried about the loss of cherished social programs. Still, seven in ten believe that social programs generally need reform. Only 27 percent, however, felt that governments genuinely wanted to improve effectiveness and efficiency through cost-cutting measures.

~ Canadians favour social investment programs that produce long-term health, security and employment opportunities. Seventy-two percent said programs that helped families with children under the age of 18 were fundamental.

PROGRAM AND POLICY STRATEGIES TO HELP CHILDREN

While considering the implications of broader social policy strategies, it is also important to look at the range of program options designed to reach children and their parents. According to Dan Offord, there are four strategies that can be employed: building civic vitality, and investing in a mixture of universal, targeted and clinical programs. **8**

— **Building civic vitality**. The strength of the social networks within communities and the commitment of its members to care for one another influence children's prospects for healthy development. "Civic vitality, or a 'community's social capital' provides a core of social resources that can support and protect children as they mature." **9** It assumes for each child the full participation in community life.

— **Universal programs**. In these initiatives all children (and their families), located in Canada or in a geographic area or setting, receive the benefit. A characteristic of universal programs is that individual families do not seek help and no one is singled out for the intervention. An obvious advantage to this approach is that there is no labelling or stigmatization of any members of a population.

— **Targeted programs**. In a targeted program, individual families and their children do not seek help. Children are identified as needing additional supports because it is determined that they are at increased risk for future problems. Targeted programs can be established based on two strategies:

identifying groups of children based on characteristics outside the child (for example, the family lives in public housing); or identifying a high-risk sample of children because they themselves have distinguishing characteristics (such as mild antisocial behaviour).

— **Clinical programs**. The major characteristic of clinical programs is that the family perceives the child as having a problem and seeks help from a psychiatrist, psychologist, social worker or other clinical professionals. But the clinical enterprise can never play a major role in promoting the optimal social and emotional health of children and youth: it is much too expensive, there are difficulties with obtaining adequate coverage of a population and the results can be discouraging.

It is important to note that effective programs at all four levels are needed. The absence of programs at one level will affect the success of a program at another level. For instance, the effectiveness of clinical programs aimed at treating children with emotional and behavioural problems will be severely curtailed if the communities in which the children live are disorganized with little social capital and lack of universal programs in such areas as skill development in the arts and sports. Conversely, programs at different levels can have synergistic effects on each other. For example, an initiative to treat youth with drug problems will have a greater chance of success if it is occurring in a community where there are effective universal programs aimed at curbing the availability of illegal drugs for youth.

> "Unfortunately, a number of successful programs don't last. We need to look carefully at why they stop functioning in order to learn more about how we can maintain successful programs over time, or how we can maintain their most successful components." **13**
>
> Dan Offord

Clearly, there are trade-offs among investments in the civic vitality of communities, and investments in clinical, targeted and universal programs. All four strategies are needed to maintain and improve the physical, social and emotional health of Canada's children. The optimal mix of these approaches will change as knowledge accumulates about effectiveness and costs of various benefits and program interventions. But as Offord points out, "it is critical that these programs ensure that children have equal access, equal participation, and equitable outcomes. Thus, the true meaning of universality." When describing the term "equitable outcomes," Offord likes to use the example of a ballet dancer. "We are all born with certain talents and capabilities. Some people have the talent to become ballet dancers and a lot don't — so I'm not saying that everybody in Canada should be given ballet lessons.

"But, if we are to achieve equitable outcomes, that means that every child who has the talent to become a Karen Kain or a John Alleyn has as much of a chance to fulfil that dream as any other child with a similar talent — regardless of family income, race, gender and other factors that tend to reduce opportunity. There should be the same range of outcomes for sports and arts activities for boys and girls, rich and poor, immigrant and non-immigrant."

To achieve that kind of equity, there has to be equal access to opportunities and equal participation in those opportunities. "I think Canadians still cherish the principles of fairness and equity," says Offord. "And I believe that equitable outcomes for all of Canada's children and youth should be our ultimate goal." **10**

VOLUNTARISM AND GOVERNMENT

A popular view of community, especially in the United States, focuses on networks of voluntary association, people helping each other. This view's adherents perceive social service systems as impediments to building community. Their attitude is, in part, a reaction to the tendency of large, centrally managed systems to suffer from hardening of the institutional arteries. In some cases, it is also a reaction against being labelled as a person or group "at risk" or "in need." The danger in this view, however, is that it reduces the idea of community to neighbour helping neighbour. This is not a bad thing — it's just not enough.

Many of the most successful community efforts in Canada incorporate both voluntary associations of people working together and community agencies funded by public dollars. For this collaboration to work well, the social service systems, of which these local agencies are a part, must adapt to what the community defines as its priorities, rather than the other way around. We need a framework that respects the contribution from each of the partners.

The next chapter describes a wide range of innovative community initiatives across Canada. However, to illustrate some of the basic elements of effective community action we can look at an initiative under way in rural Newfoundland.

NEWFOUNDLAND'S PORT AU PORT COMMUNITY EDUCATION INITIATIVE

In the early days of what is now Newfoundland's Port au Port Community Education Initiative, the impetus for community action was youth. There was not enough local economic opportunity to offer much of a future for many young people living in the 25 small communities that make up Port au Port on the southwest coast. Many youths were not finishing high school. There was heavy reliance on income security programs and a high proportion of teen mothers.

Concerns were raised by parents, educators and community leaders. The Port au Port Community Development Association formed a committee to explore underlying issues. The partnerships fostered through this process resulted in curriculum focused on developing new sources of economic strength in the region, and the Pathfinder Alternative Learning Centre for mature students and young people having trouble adjusting to regular school.

Today, the Port au Port initiative is involved in establishing resource programs for parents and their preschool children in schools around the area. The people of Port au Port realize there is an important relationship between what happens to children as infants and toddlers and the adults they become. Children who are given the best chance for good development will have a better chance to adapt to the changing economic and social demands of the next century. They will form stronger families themselves.

"The resource programs are designed to promote healthy children and healthy parenting, and to foster an appreciation of the critical role of education," says Beverley Kirby, director of the Community Education Initiative. **E4** "We believe you have to look at the whole picture. And you can't start too early. We have a prenatal nutrition program with food supplements and 'resource' moms to help women have healthy babies. We have a literacy program that encourages parents to read to their young children.

"Our partners in the school board, social services and the economic development association have all deliberately stepped outside their mandates to make these things happen. They have the foresight to see that life is not divided up by departmental rules. These babies are going to be going to school in a few years. If they aren't ready to learn, they will be more likely to have trouble in school, and our community will end up where we started — with our youth dropping out, not able to find work, going on assistance.

"We are painting a picture," says Kirby, "and we are trying to paint everyone in the community into this picture. We want there to be opportunities for everyone."

CONCLUSION

Children depend on their communities for many of the things they need to grow up healthy and competent. With limited resources, Canada has to make some hard choices. Ensuring that the needs of children are met will require some innovative solutions, based at the community level and supported through government policies and practices. The following chapter takes a look at some promising community-based approaches.

SECOND CHANCES 🔵

Roxanne's second chance started with a parenting course given in her home community on the southwest coast of Newfoundland, in an area called Port au Port, with a population of 8,000 people scattered across 25 small towns.

A teen mom who had dropped out of school, Roxanne was recently separated, with two toddlers. Roxanne took the parenting program to get advice about raising her kids. She mentioned to the school guidance counsellor who ran the program that she wished she could finish high school.

Six years later, Roxanne can look back with pride on what she has achieved with the support and encouragement of the Port au Port community. She completed the credits she needed for her high school diploma at the Pathfinder Alternative Learning Centre, which provides alternative educational opportunities for adults and for youth at risk of dropping out.

She thought at the time that getting through high school would be "the end-all and be-all." Going on in the education system seemed "too far out of reach." But after high school, other opportunities were offered through federal and provincial training and transition programs. Work placements provided useful experience. She took an entrepreneurship workshop promoting local enterprise and self-reliance. And then she attended a business administration course at Westviking College.

Throughout this period, Roxanne benefited from the partnerships developed by the Port au Port Community Education Initiative, a collaboration of agencies dedicated to promoting lifelong learning and community development — and helping families like Roxanne's.

After graduating from the two-year college program, Roxanne worked for a year as a liaison officer for the Community Education Initiative. Now she is expanding her work experience in Alberta. Beverley Kirby, director of the education initiative, is sorry to see another talented and energetic young person leave the community. But she is convinced Roxanne will be back — maybe even to start her own business in Port au Port.

The future looks a lot different for Roxanne and her son and daughter, now aged 9 and 10. She has proven something important to herself and her children. She graduated with her kids cheering her on. "I did it for myself and for my children. I wanted them to see that there's more to life."

ENDNOTES

1. Garbarino, 1995, p. 23-24
2. Putnam, 1993
3. Putnam, 1993, p. 159
4. Putnam, 1993, p. 88
5. Maxwell, 1996, presentation to National Conference of the Community Foundations of Canada
6. Peters, 1995
7. Bouchard, 1987 in Garbarino, 1990
8. Offord, in press
9. Canadian Council on Social Development, 1996, p. 33
10. Offord, interview

EXHIBIT ENDNOTES

E1. White, 1997
E2. Torjman, 1997
E3. Offord, interview
E4. Kirby, interview
E5. Roxanne (participant in the Port au Port Community Education Initiative)

SECTION III
WE CAN MAKE
A DIFFERENCE

Chapter 10
COMMUNITIES IN ACTION

Across Canada, communities are responding to the challenge of providing quality social environments for children, youth and families. Hundreds of unique community-based initiatives are under way, building collaborative efforts based on local assets and wisdom, and mobilizing to meet the defined needs of their children. This chapter consists of profiles of a sampling of these projects from across the country. (For information on how to get started in your community, see the box on pages 132–133).

Representatives of most of the initiatives in this chapter attended a national symposium on community action held in 1995 which focused on how to support effective collaborative efforts at the community level. Participants stressed the need for communities to be brought into the circle of power and decision making, rather than being left on the outside looking in. They talked about the importance of putting children and families at the centre. ❶

Community activists and civil servants at the symposium agreed on the need to spread the word about the models that are working in some communities, and the ingredients that make them work. They said that there needs to be recognition that:

~ communities must be involved at the front end, before the plans and terms of reference are drafted and budgets set;

~ communities need planning and decision-making authority in the projects in their neighbourhoods, not just advisory roles;

~ there is potential for redesign of systems from the community level "up" (the reverse of the traditional "top-down") if the will is there to let it happen; and

~ community activists and non-government agencies often feel threatened and frustrated by the imposition of rigid government guidelines and sectoral funding streams.

Participants also noted that researchers and community groups would benefit from finding ways to work more closely together. They called for researchers to engage in more community-based work, and for community activists to involve researchers at the developmental stages of their projects.

> "Our primary purpose is to promote community action. The communities hold the key to change. The job of governments and Aboriginal organizations is primarily that of support and facilitation. The evidence of the past 50 years has taught that the interventions of outside agencies into Aboriginal affairs, well intentioned or otherwise, cannot provide effective answers to the persistent problems of personal and cultural survival." **E1**
>
> Royal Commission on Aboriginal Peoples

COMMUNITY ACTIONS

The Good Food Box Program ❷

The Good Food Box Program is a relatively modest but successful community project that started in Kingston, Ontario in 1995. The Kingston project is characterized by:

~ useful, understandable information highlighting issues of concern;

~ grass-roots neighbourhood involvement;

~ good ideas that build on community strengths;

~ service providers willing to cooperate and even stretch official mandates and bureaucratic boundaries;

~ use of available resources, including private and public space;

~ financial support when and where it's needed;

~ volunteers; and

~ commitment.

The Good Food Box provides fresh fruits and vegetables to families in the north of the city, an historically low-income area with a high percentage of residents on social assistance. The project grew out of research data presented to community residents and service providers on babies born in 1988 and their families. The survey found many families' diets did not include regular servings of fresh fruit and vegetables and pointed to a lack of overall quality of food to meet children's needs.

A small group of community residents developed the idea of the Good Food Box. They looked at what had been done in other places and what their options were locally. They approached a local wholesale fruit and vegetable dealer who agreed to make monthly deliveries of fresh produce. A local school consented to provide space to sort and organize the produce. The group decided to open up participation to anyone, not just low-income families.

In eight months, the project grew to include 435 families and various neighbourhood distribution sites. The space in the local school became too small, so central delivery and sorting moved to a church basement. All labour is done by volunteers. The wholesaler delivers the produce to the church where volunteers sort and organize the boxes. It takes a whole morning. If any of the neighbourhood distribution sites don't have transportation, a volunteer driver delivers the boxes.

Each family is connected to a site near their home. The family pays $2 for a plastic food box. On the third of each month, a family also pays $15 to their local distribution site, and on the fifteenth of the month, they pick up a food box. Each box contains over 25 pounds of bananas, apples, oranges, cantaloupes, potatoes, carrots, onions, green peppers, lettuce, broccoli, cucumbers, mushrooms and other seasonal fruit. A smaller box is available for people who live alone.

The local North Kingston Community Health Centre provided some seed money when the project started. It holds the bank account for the Good Food Box, but has little involvement in the actual operation. Charlotte Rosenbaum, ❷ the executive director of the health centre, is very clear about who should get the credit for the success of this project — the community. "It is based on community initiative and community resources," says Rosenbaum. North Kingston residents are running it. It is an achievement that is a real source of pride for them. For some projects, out-side resources are not needed and not wanted. This is one that belongs to the community."

A group of volunteers is working on a newsletter to go with the Good Food Box and on special boxes for pregnant women and for families with different ethnic tastes. Their flyer is being translated into Chinese, Spanish, French and Portuguese.

The North Kingston Good Food Box Program received expertise and public funding through the Better Beginnings, Better Futures Project, a prevention demonstration program and research project operating in 8 com-munities around the province. ❸ The $2,000 in seed money for the Good Food Box came from the North Kingston Community Health Centre and Better Beginnings for Kingston Children, a publicly funded initiative.

"Better Beginnings is responsible for creating fertile ground for resi-dents to take on the Good Food Box project," says Rosenbaum. "People were given information about their children in language they could understand and use. Families were concerned that more children would be undernour-ished with the cuts in welfare rates. So they did something about it. We have not ended poverty in Kingston, but our kids are eating better and our com-munity is stronger for the commitment people have made to this project."

Just $2,000 in seed money is having an enormous payoff in terms of better nutrition for kids and families in North Kingston. The Good Food Box illustrates how communities can help themselves with the school, church, local business or the health centre providing the kind of support that is requested, not imposed.

Meadow Lake Tribal Council

In northwestern Saskatchewan, the Meadow Lake Tribal Council is painting its own community picture. Nine First Nations got together in 1981 to form a partnership to work toward a shared vision of healthy individuals, families and communities.

Ray Ahenakew, executive director of the Tribal Council, described its vision this way: "If we wish to become economically self-reliant and self-sufficient, and if we wish to become emotionally and spiritually healthy, and if we wish to live in peace and harmony with our brothers and sisters in Canada and with our physical environment, then we must find our own way home. By this I mean we must rediscover our traditional values — of caring, sharing and living in harmony — and bring them into our daily lives and practices." **4**

This holistic view of how First Nations can "find their way home" inspired the Council to combine economic development, child care and child care training, healing and wellness, parent and child education and other strategies into a comprehensive approach to community health and family support. This strategy was based on consultations with members of the First Nations.

Emphasis has been placed on using the community's own human resources, wherever possible. Community elders have been active in helping to design the Indian Child Care Program, which was developed in partnership with the University of Victoria's School of Child and Youth Care.

Autonomy is an important theme for Meadow Lake. The First Nations have assumed responsibility for their schools. The Council is negotiating to achieve recognition of Aboriginal self-government.

Meadow Lake not only recognizes the strength of community and the importance of intergenerational support, it also has a view to the longer term and recognizes the link between wealth and health. Its 20-year economic plan combines the needs and values of the communities with market information on the economic sectors, in particular those related to natural resources. Meadow Lake has identified a number of projects in forestry, mining, energy, agriculture and the service industry where it can create significant profits and employment opportunities.

Montreal's 1,2,3 Go!

In 1993, a group of concerned citizens developed a proposal for giving young kids in Montreal's poorest neighbourhoods a good start in life. Centraide of Greater Montreal undertook to support the group's proposal, and within a few months a project took shape around one objective and six guiding principles.

The objective of 1,2,3 Go! is to mobilize the necessary material, intellectual, social and political resources to help communities (neighbourhoods or villages) to develop and sustain a culture that is concerned with the well-being and development of their 0- to 3-year-olds. Hence, the name "1,2,3 Go!" The project's guiding principles are to:

~ mobilize the community;

~ promote concerted action by local institutions, services and citizens;

~ reach out to all children and families;

~ provide direct services to the children;

~ encourage parent participation; and

~ assure the quality of the project's interventions and practitioners.

In early 1995, six neighbourhoods were approached and invited to adopt the 1,2,3 Go! initiative. Each of the neighbourhoods set up a task force to support the initiative's implementation. While respecting the autonomy and creativity of the neighbourhoods, the project involves as many neighbourhood residents as possible, as well as the various groups that already work with young children and their families to maximize concerted community action. Some of the outcomes within the neighbourhoods include:

~ More than 600 parents and other residents living in the six neighbourhoods have been actively involved in identifying the priorities around which to frame their neighbourhood action plan. Parents are initially contacted by going door to door, meeting them informally at kindergartens, social service offices and in the parks, and by organizing small coffee gatherings in neighbourhood houses.

~ In the neighbourhood of St-Michel, a group of parents and other community partners have organized a cooperative arrangement to buy nutritious foods such as fresh fruits and vegetables; hired a street worker to ensure the safety and cleanliness of a local park; and will organize a parent centre to provide quality early childhood education and respite care for parents who need a break.

~ In North Montreal, where there are few resources within the neighbourhood, parents and other community partners got together to organize a family resource centre that centrally houses medical services, child care and social services, and hired two mothers to help coordinate it.

~ In Laval, more than 500 people came out to a community celebration of the unveiling of this neighbourhood's 1,2,3 Go! action plan.

According to Camil Bouchard, a child psychologist at the University of Quebec at Montreal and one of the creators of 1,2,3 Go!, "The aim of 1,2,3 Go! is to empower communities to create a secure, warm, supportive and generous environment for local children and their parents. This project is not entirely original: it's based upon previous North American early childhood prevention and stimulation programs. But it does add some new elements to those previous programs. For instance, 1,2,3 Go!:

~ is funded by the private sector;

~ is heavily dependent upon volunteer participation at every level of its organization; and

~ has a strong research component to help measure results." [5]

Making Community Happen: The Dufferin Mall

Toronto's Dufferin Mall is just one example of a business enterprise that decided to get involved in the community. It chose to become a catalyst for good things to happen, particularly for young people in the community surrounding the mall.

The Dufferin Mall, operated by Marathon Realty, is located in Toronto's west end. It serves a diverse community of some 60 ethnocultural groups speaking 40 languages. A few years ago, the mall became the focus of criminal activity involving youth gangs, drug dealing, chronic shoplifting, robbery and even a murder.

Businesses in the mall were suffering, but so was the community. The choice, according to mall manager David Hall, was to turn the shopping centre into a fortress or do something creative to counter the wider social problem that was spilling into the shopping centre. Hall opted for a strategy that extended far beyond the immediate, short-term interest of the mall's tenants.

Mall management created a community newspaper and provided start-up money. It invited social agencies to set up in a storefront to provide youth counselling services. It formed partnerships with local schools so education programs could be offered at the mall, including school re-entry programs for dropouts and an accredited marketing course for students taking jobs in mall retail outlets. The mall shared a youth worker with a local community centre. It also provided funds to improve a playground across the street, got involved in a school breakfast program and sponsored a youth theatre group. The list of programs and activities is long and is always evolving in response to community needs.

Today, Dufferin Mall is thriving. Mall developers, retailers, educators and social service workers from around the world visit to find out its secret.

"We give people in the community the resources they need to run programs they believe in. Our philosophy is simple — the better the quality of life of the community, the better the business environment. If drugs and youth alienation are destroying a community, they will destroy business as well. It is therefore incumbent on business to make improvements in the community. We believe kids are an asset, not a liability, and a lot of our time is spent proving this out. The results are obviously worth it." **E2**

David Hall, Manager, Dufferin Mall

The Federal Government's Community Action Program for Children

The Community Action Program for Children (CAPC) is one of a series of steps taken by the federal government in response to the United Nations Convention on the Rights of the Child. CAPC funds community coalitions to establish and deliver services that address the developmental needs of children 0 to 6 years old whose health is at risk.

There are currently about 500 ongoing projects in over 300 communities reaching:

~ children living in low-income families;

~ children living in teenage-parent families;

~ children experiencing developmental delays, social, emotional or behavioural problems;

~ abused and neglected children;

~ immigrant and refugee children; and

~ Métis, Inuit and First Nations children living off-reserve.

The kinds of community-based projects organized with CAPC funding include parent training, home visits, one-on-one child development intervention, nutrition counselling, mobile unit to isolated and rural areas, moms and tots programs, headstart programs, collective kitchens and traditional Aboriginal healing programs.

Health Canada estimates that 28,000 children and parents or caregivers visit CAPC projects each week and project volunteers donate nearly 30,000 hours each month.

SCHOOLS IN COMMUNITIES AND COMMUNITIES IN SCHOOLS

Community In Schools

The Community In Schools movement, active in Canada as well as in the United States, Britain and Ireland, seeks to inspire and mobilize caring communities within schools to ensure that all children and youth can learn, stay in school and prepare for life. Its basic principles summarize much of what recent research confirms about what children need and the important role of community:

"EVERY CHILD NEEDS AND DESERVES:

A PERSONAL, ONE-ON-ONE RELATIONSHIP WITH A CARING ADULT.

A SAFE PLACE TO LEARN AND GROW.

A MARKETABLE SKILL TO USE UPON GRADUATION.

A CHANCE TO GIVE BACK TO PEERS AND COMMUNITY." [6]

When professionals, service providers, parents and volunteers work collaboratively with schools, children are surrounded with a new community made up of adults who care about them.

Changes may occur in a child's life because of this caring community, including increased motivation and self-esteem, increased literacy, reduced dropout rates and reduced rates of school violence. Ultimately more productive members of society are created. **7**

Sir William Macdonald Elementary School

Vancouver's Sir William Macdonald Elementary School is trying to encourage parents to become part of the school community and to make the school part of their community. It has required more than simply opening its doors: many Aboriginal parents in the neighbourhood don't have good memories of school and aren't keen to visit one again.

"The reality is that people have been betrayed and hurt in the past," says Holly Paxton, a neighbourhood assistant with the inner city project of the Vancouver School Board. "We use Aboriginal healing circles and other traditional ways to help parents liberate themselves. By liberation, we mean freeing from our hearts some of our experiences so that we can come closer in understanding and work together for future generations." **8**

Sunset Park Public School

North Bay, Ontario is a typical Canadian city with 55,000 people. Like many communities, it's trying to grapple with the many problems of modern life. And so are its children. Debbie Wintle, a counsellor at Sunset Park Public School, is on the frontlines with those children. The elementary school, which goes up to Grade 6, has set up a "comfort couch" reserved for children who are upset, anxious, afraid or in trouble. It's there for children who need someone to talk to in private — someone they can trust.

Wintle listens to kids trying to deal with some tough stuff: family conflict, death of a relative, fights with other children, suicide, illness, separation and divorce, anger, depression, stealing, family violence, substance abuse, emotional abuse and anxiety.

"I work with kids on things like anger management, tolerance for other people, friendship and learning to like yourself," says Wintle. "I've had some of the children say to me, 'This is what we really need to learn. Yes, we need to learn to read and write. But this is what we need to live by to survive.'" 9

Some of these children have already seen a lot of strife despite their tender years.

~ The girl who called 9-1-1 when her stepfather had too much to drink and assaulted her mom.

~ The girl who wanted to end her life because she couldn't think of a reason to go on after her family moved and she lost her friends and supportive teachers at her old school.

~ The angry boy who came from another school where he missed 75 days on suspension the year before.

Sunset Park is a pilot project in community development for the Nipissing Board of Education. Sunset Park is not a traditional school; it plays a larger role in the community. The school is a focal point where the community is invited to gather to support children and families.

School principal Rick Ferron is a soft-spoken man who likes to give other people the limelight. He is most comfortable talking about the supportive staff and parents' group at the school and the cooperation coming from the many community organizations involved in programs at the school.

"Our most important partnership is with parents. We make sure they know that. We also have great organizational partners," Ferron says. "Those partners include Nipissing Public Health, the Nipissing Children's Aid Society, Nipissing Children's Mental Health, the Optimists Club, the Herbert A. Bruce Chapter of the International Order of Daughters of the Empire, Canadore College in North Bay and Cambrian College in Sudbury, as well as various private and anonymous benefactors. The working committee for this *Community Project for Children* is in discussion with two national foundations for support and backing to expand the initiative into the broader community of North Bay." 10

Beyond teaching in the classroom, Sunset Park has a parent-child drop-in centre with a counsellor and a public health nurse, a clothing program for parents and children, co-op placements for high school credit for teen mothers, self-worth support groups, a food and nutrition program, attention-deficit hyperactivity workshops and peer mediation training. There is a parent-child coordinator on staff part time who not only organizes activities for groups of children, but also provides counselling, crisis intervention and referrals for children needing additional help.

"All this community outreach doesn't change the school's ultimate responsibility for turning out competent students ready to go on to higher learning," says Ferron. "It doesn't even make our job, as educators, easier. Our staff is here 'til all hours. But I believe we're more successful helping our kids to learn because we are dealing with them as human beings, not just students in a classroom, and because we're drawing in from the community far more resources for kids than we could ever provide on our own."

Ferron says the children's academic test results on system-wide assessments in mathematics and language arts are very good, considering the deep social needs of many of the children. The youngest children at the school show the greatest promise because they have had the benefit of the school's caring and supportive environment earlier in their development. Test scores tend to improve after students have been at the school for a few years. However, in some Grade 6 classes, only about 20 percent of the children have been at Sunset Park since Grade 3. Parents move around, often to find work, and their kids move with them.

Part of the school's strength is its emphasis on personal involvement and earning students' trust. Vice-principal John Stephens knows every child by name and every family. He says the success of the school is probably not told by the statistics: "It's our stories that tell how we are doing." **11**

~ The 8-year-old who is smiling and learning after a period of suicidal despair.

~ The twins who arrived at school essentially unable to talk. With daily individual attention from a college student in early childhood education, they are now speaking and learning some vocabulary. They can count and are making progress.

~ The recently separated mother of two who said that her daughter in senior kindergarten is doing well: "She has blossomed here. She has courage. The school has been so supportive of us."

~ The mother of a son diagnosed with attention-deficit hyperactivity who raves about the support and freedom she has been given to carry on a parent-support group.

~ The dad who had been working three part-time jobs and couldn't make ends meet. He wasn't told that the family Christmas dinner came from a discreet donations drive at the school. Suddenly in February, he showed up at the school to offer to help with work around the property in the spring. "He must have found out. It was his way of saying thanks," says Stephens.

GETTING STARTED IN YOUR COMMUNITY: A CHECKLIST

Those communities that try to identify the needs of their children, and develop comprehensive plans to address those needs, are more likely to find effective solutions. But there is no one "blueprint" for successful community action. Each community has its own particular needs and its unique combination of resources.

Building on community-based "success stories" and the latest research findings and best practices can help lead the way but, in the end, it is the needs of children in your community, your community's collective assets and the possibilities for community-wide collaboration, that will help define your community's particular goals and implementation strategies.

The following are a few questions to keep in mind:

▲ Who are the key people in the community concerned about the well-being of children, the community's social environment and the local economy? For example, individuals who are:

> currently involved in caring, educating and providing services for children;

> researchers and experts in child development and social policy;

> leaders in local politics, business, labour and the media; and

> young people, community activists, members of parent organizations and volunteers?

▲ What is the best forum for bringing these partners together? For example:

> organizing a task force set up by the mayor's office, by municipal leaders or by a planning association;

> building a coalition of community-based organizations that serves children, youth and families;

> bringing together a dedicated group of community members who have potential access to resources, research and expertise; or

> developing a "child-friendly" community effort?

▲ How can you effectively use data to guide your efforts? In other words, how do you go about measuring how well your community's children are doing and assessing the community assets at your disposal?

> Who in the community collects data on children; for example, a district health council, school boards, a child care association, a university, municipal/regional government, etc.?

> Who can you recruit to help pull this information together or to look at developing new indicators to help measure the well-being and competence of children in your community?

> What are some of the assets within your community, such as voluntary networks, service systems that are open to change and collaboration, equity of opportunities and outcomes for children, and financial and in-kind sources of support?

▲ How can your group develop an "action plan" that lays out steps to improve outcomes for your community's children? Based on the assessment of both the key strengths and weaknesses in your community:

> What do you want to achieve or, in other words, what problems do you want to address?

> How can you make the best use of the expertise that exists in your community?

> What are the most practical next steps? What are some of the issues that require more long-term planning?

> What kinds of indicators or benchmarks can you use that will show whether you achieved your objectives? For example, what is the percentage of low birth weight babies, and how many children are assessed to be ready to learn when they arrive in Grade 1?

▲ How can you build broad-based support for your action plan?

> What are the key messages you would like to convey to the community as a whole?

> What practical steps can you recommend to people who might be interested in getting involved in the community? For example, targeting individual members of: NEIGHBOURHOODS • LABOUR • BUSINESS • GOVERNMENT • NON-GOVERNMENTAL ORGANIZATIONS, CHARITIES AND RELIGIOUS CONGREGATIONS • PROFESSIONAL ORGANIZATIONS

▲ Who can help you develop and implement a public relations and media strategy?

ENDNOTES

1. Healthy Child Development Project, 1995. The information on community initiatives included in this chapter is drawn from Healthy Children, Healthy Communities and the National Symposium on Community Action for Children, and from personal interviews conducted for this publication or related published articles as noted.

2. Rosenbaum, interview

3. Peters & Russell, 1996

4. Fanjoy, 1994, p. 17

5. Bouchard, interview

6. Milliken, interview

7. Sylva 1994; King & Peart, 1990, Toronto Board of Education, 1989

8. Paxton, interview

9. Wintle, interview

10. Ferron, interview

11. Stephens, interview

EXHIBIT ENDNOTES

E1. Royal Commission on Aboriginal Peoples, 1995, p. 89

E2. Hall, interview

Chapter 11
FINDING SOLUTIONS AND TAKING ACTION

f we are serious about supporting optimal child development in Canada, there's a lot of work ahead.

The task isn't simple. The government debt problem of the 1980s and early 1990s has forced changes in the way Canadians think about social programs. While most Canadians remain committed to social programs, especially those that benefit children, they are also demanding those that are more effective and efficient. At the same time, with devolution and decentralization of government, there are shifts in the delivery of services.

The problems facing children can't be solved at one level of society or by one department or institution. Although governments must provide leadership, they alone cannot resolve all the problems facing children. In some cases, there isn't the money. In others, governments may not be the best institution for dealing with the problem. However, it's foolish to think that volunteers and community groups alone can solve the daunting problems facing children. Children and parents will benefit most when all levels of society work in concert to strengthen families and tackle their problems.

No matter who sponsors programs and initiatives, we need to evaluate the success and failures of our efforts — at all levels and by all sectors — to support children and families. It is important to know how we are using money and other resources, and the actual impact of these investments. What do we know about the best way to organize health services, social programs and schools to increase opportunities for as many children as possible? We need solid information to guide our decisions, and to provide us with a better understanding of how our children are doing and what's making a difference. (See the discussion of different social policy strategies in "Community Is Us.")

STEP 1: USING KNOWLEDGE

As this book illustrates, we are learning more about the factors that give children a fair chance to develop to their full potential. For example, we have learned that physical health is related to income and the social and physical environment. Making sure that all of Canada's children have what they need in their earliest years to fully develop is one key way to prevent health problems later in life.

In social services, there is now a trend to rethink current approaches in terms of outcomes. People are looking at what we have done to support children and families, for example, and asking some fundamental questions, like: "How much of a difference are we making? Does a non-integrated system of services, each designed to address a specific problem, really work? If it doesn't, what will?"

In education, there is a growing emphasis on linking schools, parents and communities more closely together and making schools a focal point for improving outcomes for children and youth. At the provincial and local levels, government ministries responsible for child-related issues are finding ways to coordinate efforts around improving outcomes while reducing overall costs. New partnerships within government and with the private sector are being forged.

Despite the progress so far, many of our practices, institutions and policies are currently operating on old assumptions — not on new knowledge and findings.

By using new knowledge to promote healthy development from before birth to adolescence, we will help more children to acquire the skills they need to grow up healthy and more young people to have the sense of belonging and self-esteem they need to become effective, participating members of society.

STEP 2: FROM KNOWLEDGE TO INNOVATION

The research findings discussed in *Our Promise to Children* present us with a challenge: how do we translate this knowledge into a new way of thinking and acting? We have much of what it takes to get the job done: a great deal can be accomplished through reallocation of existing resources and building the capacity within communities. We will never have all of the evidence in place to satisfy everyone — nor will we avoid mistakes along the way — but there is a growing convergence of views across Canada calling for a new approach which includes the following elements:

— **Promotion and prevention versus treatment**: We will need to focus on ways to help all children develop to their full potential, thus seeking to prevent many problems, rather than mainly addressing problems once they occur. The Laidlaw Foundation describes this as a moving away from our tendency to organize resources around the reduction of negative traits ("deficits") and toward the promotion of positive traits ("assets") and aspirations. This alone is a fundamental shift in the way we allocate resources and provide supports. ❶

— **Bridging disciplinary and sectoral boundaries:** The challenges we face in helping to raise a healthy and productive new generation are multifaceted. They require the involvement and coordination of numerous departments at all levels of government, private sector organizations and professional specialties. We will need to apply the creative ideas of people in many different sectors and disciplines. We will also need to bridge a host of barriers, such as between health care and child care, economic development and human development, and the child welfare system and the justice system.

— **Community renewal and mobilization:** Communities have a key role to play in finding their own innovative strategies for promoting optimal child development. Community leaders and members coming together to express their concern for children and their determination to do something positive will be a vital part of the solution. Schools, voluntary associations, local congregations, community organizations, business and professional groups, labour organizations and service clubs are all potential participants, along with all levels of government. Representatives of people living in disadvantaged circumstances should be essential partners.

— **Building public understanding and support:** Public awareness and understanding are important factors in helping our young people. The general public and various interest groups need to have a clearer understanding of the determinants of optimal child development, to support investments that benefit all children and to be involved in child- and youth-focused initiatives. Now is the time to build a non-partisan agenda, embraced and sustained by people from the neighbourhood to the national level.

— **Results-based approach:** When all is said and done, results are what counts. Are more children and youth growing up physically and emotionally healthy? Do they have the skills necessary to participate fully in society? How can we tell? We will need to set some goals for optimal child development which can be measured and evaluated. Communities must have the tools they need to determine priorities, set achievable goals and track outcomes.

— **Involving young people:** One of the resources we have traditionally overlooked in developing strategies for children is young people themselves. They have a lot of the questions and ideas we will need to address in promoting optimal child and youth development. Adults must consider whether we have created a culture that ignores youth until they are older — or one that encourages youth to participate and develop their citizenship skills early.

STEP 3: KEEPING SCORE

Most industrialized nations devote substantial resources to researching where they stand in economic terms. The indicators of a country's relative economic health are widely followed: much attention is paid to growth in the Gross National Product, inflation indicators and the deficit.

Keeping score on how well we are doing as a society to promote optimal child development is of no less importance to Canada. Healthy outcomes — such as physical health and child well-being — are important to everyone's future and closely connected to Canada's economic prospects.

We already track some measures of child development by keeping statistics on physical health, such as birth weights, infant mortality and childhood injuries. But tracking other indicators like cognitive development at key transition points — for example, when children enter school — will help us discover how well our young are developing to their potential.

According to Dan Offord, director of the Centre for Studies of Children at Risk in Hamilton, Ontario, "It's not just a matter of measuring what's going *wrong*, but what's going *right* for our kids." **2**

It is by no means enough to track an economic problem — for example, our rising indebtedness — without also considering what action to take to correct the situation. Similarly, we need to go beyond measuring optimal child development and examine the impact of various courses of action — ranging from policy level interventions concerning employment and income support policies to individual community programs.

The National Longitudinal Survey of Children and Youth (NLSCY) **3** is under way to help track the well-being of Canadian children over the years. Reports such as *Progress of Canada's Children* **4** and *The Health of Canada's Children* **5** will keep tabs on the successes and failures in dealing with these problems. The Centre for Studies of Children at Risk, with funding from the Atkinson Foundation, is developing and testing a community report card. (Refer to Appendix B for more information on these and other efforts to measure progress and evaluate programs and policies.)

Putting yardsticks against the lot of Canada's children is an important start. Of course, it's not sufficient by itself. As the Canadian Council on Social Development said in its 1996 report, "Measuring progress is not the same as making progress." **6**

STEP 4: LEADERSHIP AND PARTICIPATION
MAKE IT HAPPEN

It is said that information is power, but information alone does not necessarily translate into action. The catalyst for action is leadership and involvement — people who are able to see what needs doing and work with others to do it.

Significant efforts are already under way that lead us in the right direction. Examples include:

~ programs by federal government departments that promote the health and well-being of children and youth;

~ the emergence of innovative provincial-level children's initiatives that focus on inter-sectoral collaboration, community-based innovation and evaluation;

~ the growing leadership on children's issues by private foundations and the business community;

~ the ongoing work of non-governmental organizations across Canada to support the health and well-being of children, youth and families;

~ a variety of academic and research projects; and

~ of particular importance, the commitment and dedication of individuals in every region of Canada who are making a real difference in children's lives.

Ensuring the healthy development of Canada's children and youth depends largely upon people who can work together to facilitate change, build on each other's successes and work effectively across sectors. We need to bring together people to unite around a common vision, commit to making a difference and work to facilitate change.

KEEPING SCORE

Because of the importance of civic vitality to children's healthy development, it becomes important for us to learn how to measure a community's social capital, or its capacity to support children's optimal growth and development. Marvyn Novick, professor of social work at Ryerson Polytechnic University in Toronto, points out, "It is not enough to keep track of whether children merely survive or don't survive. We need to know if they are thriving. Children thrive when a community's civic health is high. Therefore, we need to keep track of the assets and liabilities within a community that we know make a difference to children and youth." **E1** In addition, measuring how well *all children* in a community are doing, rather than measuring how well *individual children* are doing, opens the door for investments in community-wide prevention strategies.

NO TIME TO SELL CHILDREN SHORT

We are in a period of acute public sector spending restraint. Canadians with innovative ideas often complain they can't get a bank loan because they're unable to produce tangible collateral and their idea will take some developmental time. Similarly, innovation and prevention in child development may be a target for cutbacks.

Government budgets are tight and there are limits to the time people can devote. That means priorities will have to be set. Money and time will need to be used effectively. Securing those resources will depend on winning the economic argument that the returns from investing in children are great. And that the long-run cost of neglect is even greater.

The Mismatch between Opportunity and Investment E2

Based on United States data, this chart demonstrates a government's tendency toward greater financial investments later in the life cycle, thereby missing the most critical opportunity to promote human competence and potential.

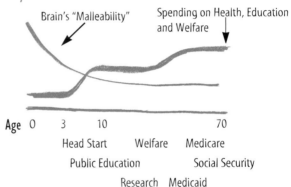

John Evans, chairman of Torstar Corporation and previous chairman of the Rockefeller Foundation, says that governments should concentrate their efforts where they can do the most good in preventing problems for children:

~ income support to maintain reasonable living standards for lower wage earners and the unemployed — families where most child development problems occur; and

~ increased spending on specific high-impact programs, such as parent counselling, quality child care, preschool enrichment and youth employment.

At the same time, communities should not depend exclusively on government efforts. Community action has to be seen as a complement to government action, not as a replacement for it. They can achieve results that governments can't if they organize community members around finding solutions at the grass-roots level. Evans says that although community action will be slow and uneven, families and children will be the major beneficiaries from programs designed to support parents and to make neighbourhoods safer. **7**

PAY NOW OR PAY LATER E3

The National Crime Prevention Council estimates that costs and expenditures associated with crime in Canada is about $46 billion annually when both system costs and costs of the results of crime are taken into account. This estimate does not include the cost of white-collar crime.

"Is crime prevention through social development a good investment in safety as well as in savings? The answer is 'yes.' For example, the Rand Corporation estimates that if we took $1 million and invested it in prison space for career criminals, this investment would prevent 60 crimes a year. If that same amount was used to monitor 12- and 13-year-old 'delinquents,' it would prevent 72 crimes a year. Further, if that million dollars was invested in incentives for young people to graduate from high school, 258 crimes a year would be prevented." **E4**

A TIME TO ACT

It's significant that so many sectors in Canadian society are now focusing their attention on the importance of investing in children. Despite government spending restraint, investing in child and youth development is on the table at the federal and provincial levels.

A lot of the new research is confirming what many Canadians would call "common sense" about raising kids. What is significant, however, is that there is now more scientific evidence that leaves less room for debate by those who oppose action. When it comes to helping kids, it's clear that:

▲ parents are the most important people in children's lives, but they need support from neighbours, relatives, communities and society; and

▲ there are enormous benefits to investing in efforts that:

~ support parents to better nurture their children;

~ provide quality care and stimulation to preschoolers; and

~ enhance the civic vitality of communities.

It's possible to apply these principles to make a difference for kids — providing parents with the kind of knowledge and support they need, and acting on what we know works in raising children. Aboriginal leader Phil Fontaine, former grand chief of the Assembly of Manitoba Chiefs and currently grand chief of the Assembly of First Nations, made an eloquent plea to get moving at the National Symposium on Community Action for Children, held in Winnipeg in 1995. He summed up the issue:

"All of our best efforts in life should be dedicated to ensuring we provide the best for our young people. They deserve nothing less. They deserve the respect and dignity and honour we expect for ourselves. Put your minds together to do what is needed for young people." [8]

Families must remain the focus of child rearing. But the family should be seen as the first of many rings of support surrounding every child in Canada. Extended families, child care programs, community centres, schools, hospitals, municipalities, and federal and provincial governments all have roles in creating a world that will nurture and sustain children. The key point is that the child is at the centre. In Canada's North, when a herd of muskox is attacked by wolves, the adults form a defensive circle around the calves, their horns turned to the enemy. Children should expect no less from their society. Society gains from every child who succeeds in life. And it pays dearly for every child who is left to the wolves.

That doesn't mean that society can guarantee that every child will succeed in life. In fact, growing up is kind of a gamble. Some will always beat the odds. However, it also makes sense to stack the odds in favour of as many children as possible, instead of betting on long-shots. The more the four determinants of healthy development — protection, relationships, opportunity and community — are in a child's favour, the greater the chance that the child will end up contributing to society as an adult instead of being dependent on it. The earlier children get their needs fulfilled, the better. Children can bounce back from a poor start. But a poor start makes it harder to reach their potential.

Communities are already doing a lot to help children, young people and families in resourceful ways. What is happening, however, is only a fraction of what could happen if Canadians put their collective will toward improving the prospects for the optimal development of children. To ensure that Canada is the best place we can make it for children to grow up well, every Canadian has a part to play. Every Canadian has a promise to keep — to our children, and to our future.

WHAT CAN YOU DO?

All of us who come into contact with kids can either support or detract from their healthy development. Are our neighbourhood streets safe? Do parents know where to turn when they need help in the demanding job of protecting and nurturing children? Do our schools provide the kind of learning that will help kids grow to their full potential and later compete in the future marketplace? Does our economy function adequately to provide jobs for parents who must support their children? Does our society practise and pass on the kind of values it promotes, such as equity, protection of the vulnerable and respect for all human beings?

If you are a parent
~ To help your child realize his or her full potential, you may want to look at the suggestions of the I Am Your Child Campaign found on pages 148-149.
~ Develop a support network, drawing on the help of relatives, friends, neighbours and community organizations.
~ Find out about the kinds of resources that exist in the community to help you, such as child care information services, family resource centres and services for children and families.
~ Get involved in your community and its civic organizations. The safety, quality and vitality of a community depends on the active involvement of its members.

If you are a member of the business community

~ Make it your business to become familiar with the latest research findings that link economic prosperity with investments in early childhood development.

~ Help make it easy for employees to find high quality child care or set up an on-site child care program.

~ Offer your employees a variety of work arrangements, including flexible work hours, part-time work or job sharing.

~ Provide local teenagers with summer or after-school internships at your company.

~ Encourage employees to volunteer in community projects, especially those in which employees can serve as tutors or mentors with individual children.

~ Provide financial donations to innovative community projects and donate in-kind support such as equipment and employee expertise.

~ Become a participant and leader in community-wide efforts designed to improve outcomes for children and youth.

If you are a government official, a professional in health and social services, a researcher or a community leader

~ Take the time to build momentum for collaboration within your area or sphere of influence. Next, begin to build connections with other departments, disciplines or organizations. We can no longer afford duplication or disjointed solutions.

~ Balance top-down influence with bottom-up innovation. Both are important and both are required. Local innovation sometimes gets stopped in its tracks by restrictions from above, or sometimes can't get off the ground because of the lack of political and government support.

~ Encourage big ideas and achievable first steps. All of us need to move beyond our comfort level with the status quo and take that first step toward change. We can either choose now to implement new strategies or wait until circumstances leave us with no other choice.

~ Look for ways to link people, programs and resources. Fortunately, in Canada there is no shortage of valuable ideas and people who want to do good. But to effectively harness this energy and commitment, we need to avoid isolation.

~ Look for measurable outcomes and accountability. A lot of resources are wasted because we fail to evaluate efforts based on their impact on children's lives. We need to move beyond the theory of what should work to the evidence of what does work. Allow the results to speak for themselves and guide your decisions. Invest in solutions proven to be effective.

~ If you are an expert in your field, serve as a resource person for your community. A rule of thumb for successful community collaboration: use your expertise to help facilitate change by working together with other community partners, not by prescribing your own "solution."

~ Keep your eyes focused on the child. It's easy to get caught up in short-term political agendas and in competition for resources and recognition. As soon as we focus on our own agendas or organizations — rather than on what's best for children — we risk becoming part of the problem and not the solution. Children deserve our clarity, and our attention to what's most important.

If you are involved in politics

~ Make public investment in child development a priority. There's ample scientific and public support for strategies that help children grow to their full potential. As research illustrates, this agenda is both cost-effective and in the best interests of Canada's economic prosperity.

~ Use the expertise of child development experts, researchers and non-governmental organizations. Often an untapped resource by government officials and politicians, these experts can provide scientific data, advice on strategic policies and programs, and garner support for your commitment to make a real difference.

~ Develop an agenda, backed by financial resources, to help communities find their own solutions.

If you're a member of the media

~ Look for human interest stories that illustrate how good programs and policies make a positive difference in children's lives.

~ Report on new research findings related to child development.

~ Give interested readers the information they need to get involved in programs at the community level.

For all of us

~ No matter where you live, there are bound to be children within reach

who are living in circumstances of risk. Research demonstrates that relationships are critical; one caring and competent adult in a child's life can make a
world of difference. Get involved with mentoring, tutoring and early childhood education programs in your community.

~ Get involved in the public debate on social issues related to children. We
can't put the blame on the government of the day if we're not willing to take
a stand ourselves. It's up to us to hold the government accountable for its
actions or inactions. Contact your elected officials at all levels of government about issues that affect children, or write a letter to the editor, or run
for the local school board, or get involved in a political campaign.

IT'S A MATTER OF VALUES

An 8-year-old girl suffering from a rare blood disease was in need of
a transfusion. But no match could be found. The girl's doctor and mother
then asked her 6-year-old brother if he would be willing to give his blood to
save his sister's life. He said he would have to think about it, and eventually
said "Okay, I'll do it." A couple of days later, the brother and sister laid down
beside one another in the hospital while the blood was successfully trans-
ferred. After a few minutes, the little boy called the doctor over to his bed
and whispered in the physician's ear, "Will I start to die right away?"

Bob Glossop, head of the Vanier Institute of the Family, recounted
this story at the Canada's Children, Canada's Future Conference held in
Ottawa in 1996. He closed his remarks by suggesting to the audience, "This
is what a child was willing to give for the sake of love. And it leaves me with
the question: 'What are we willing to give to our children for the sake of
tomorrow?' " **9**

The American child development expert, Urie Bronfenbrenner, is
well known for his tenet that what all children need is at least one person in
their life who is crazy about them. **10** Amplifying this concept to the
responsibility of society as a whole, Quebec released a report in 1991 called
Quebec: Crazy About Our Kids. **11** The report's advisory committee chair,
Camil Bouchard of the University of Quebec at Montreal, says that "the lack
of social values can be a threat to a child's well-being. This includes the
prevalence of a 'me, myself and I' attitude, the still quite popular belief that

THE FIRST YEARS LAST FOREVER — TIPS FOR PARENTS AND CAREGIVERS

New brain research tells us that the first three years of life are a critical period in a child's development. Early experiences help determine the child's brain structure — shaping the way he or she learns, thinks and behaves for the rest of his or her life. The I Am Your Child Campaign is a public awareness project coordinated by the Family and Work Institute in New York. **E5** Dedicated to making early childhood development a top priority, this campaign is led in Canada by the Canadian Institute of Child Health. The campaign has developed 10 basic guidelines to help parents and caregivers raise healthier, happier children.

▲ Be warm, loving and responsive.

We know that children's early attachments affect the way their brains work and grow. When children receive warm, responsive care, they are more likely to feel safe and secure with the adults who take care of them. Researchers call these strong relationships "secure attachments"; they are the basis of the child's future relationships.

▲ Respond to the child's cues and clues.

The clues and cues that infants send are the sounds they make, the ways they move and the facial expressions they use. Children become securely attached when parents and other caregivers try to read these signals and respond with sensitivity. There are simple steps parents can take to build trust in their young children: the child smiles and someone smiles back; they are upset and someone comforts them; they are hungry and someone feeds them. Parents who respond to their children's needs for attention, as well as quiet time, help their children form secure attachments.

▲ Talk, sing and read to your child.

Telling stories about daily events, reading children's books aloud, singing songs about the people and places your child knows, describing what is happening during daily routines — these give your child a solid basis for later learning.

▲ Establish routines and rituals.

Daily routines and rituals associated with pleasurable feelings are reassuring for children. Teach your child to know his or her nap time by performing a routine that the child can learn to recognize. For example, sing a song and close the curtains every day when it's time for a nap. Or, before bed, read a story to your child. These routines help children learn what to expect from their environment, and how to understand the world around them a little more easily. Children who have safe and predictable interactions with others have also been found to do better in school later on.

▲ Encourage safe exploration and play.

As infants grow, they begin to explore the world beyond their caregivers. Parents should encourage this exploration and be receptive when the child needs to return to them for questions and security. While many of us think of learning as simply acquiring facts, children actually learn through playing.

▲ Make television watching selective.

Television by itself can't teach an infant language, and it can't teach a child how to communicate. Be selective and involved in your children's television habits. Don't use TV as a babysitter. Whenever possible, sit and watch programs together with your child and talk about what you're viewing.

▲ Use discipline as an opportunity to teach.

As children explore their ever-expanding world, they need limits and consistent, loving adult supervision. Studies reveal that the way in which adults provide discipline is crucial to their children's later development. Many approaches to setting limits can work, as long as they are intended to help and teach children rather than to punish them. Never hit or shake a child. Brain research has shown that these forms of "discipline" can have long-term negative effects.

▲ Recognize that each child is unique.

Children grow at different rates. Their feelings about themselves largely reflect parents' and caregivers' attitudes toward them. Parents and caregivers who are sensitive to their particular child's cues help them build positive self-esteem.

▲ Choose quality child care and stay involved.

To make a good child care choice, visit and observe how providers respond and interact with the children in their care. Seek a provider who responds warmly to your child's needs. Select someone who cares about children, is eager to learn about their development, and will give children individual attention and engage them in creative play and exploration. Find a setting that is clean and safe, and carefully check the provider's references.

▲ Take care of yourself.

Parents and caregivers need care, too. When you are exhausted, preoccupied, irritable or depressed, you will probably have a harder time meeting the needs of young children. When you feel overwhelmed, take care of yourself. Reach out and get some help. Families, friends, neighbours, family physicians, child care providers and others can assist you in fostering your child's healthy development.

children are the property of parents and the myth that children are not yet 'people' in their own right." **12**

Imagine a Canada that is "crazy about our kids" — a country that makes caring for its children the highest of priorities. As *Our Promise to Children* illustrates, making such a commitment is supported by our new understanding of what makes a society productive and prosperous. But ultimately, investing in Canada's children is a matter of values.

Living up to the values of justice and fairness that we espouse — as individuals and as a society — makes the difference between wishes and reality, between talking and action, between self-interest and caring, between making promises and keeping promises. But most of all, living up to the values we espouse makes all the difference in the world to Canada's children. That's a promise we can't afford to break.

ENDNOTES

1. Shields, 1993
2. Offord, interview
3. Human Resources Development Canada and Statistics Canada, 1996
4. Canadian Council on Social Development, 1996
5. Canadian Institute of Child Health, 1994A
6. Canadian Council on Social Development, 1996, p. 57
7. Evans, 1996
8. Fontaine, 1995, presentation at National Symposium on Community Action for Children, November 1995
9. Glossop, 1996, speech at Canada's Children, Canada's Future Conference, November 25-27, 1996
10. Bronfenbrenner, 1979
11. Quebec Ministry of Health and Social Services, 1991
12. Bouchard, interview

EXHIBIT ENDNOTES

E1. Novick, interview
E2. Perry, 1997
E3. National Crime Prevention Council, 1997
E4. National Crime Prevention Council, 1997, p. 6
E5. Family and Work Institute, 1997

Appendix A
CANADA'S KIDS: THRIVING OR JUST SURVIVING?
New Research Tells the Epic Tale of Our Nation's Children and Their Families in the 1990s

T he Vanier Institute of the Family, in its March 1997 edition of *Transition*, provided a synopsis of the state of Canada's children called "Canada's Kids: Thriving or Just Surviving?" It is based on the analysis of two publications: the Canadian Council on Social Development's *The Progress of Canada's Children 1996* and Statistics Canada's *Growing Up in Canada*. Both draw on many sources, especially the first results from an ongoing federal government initiative called the National Longitudinal Survey on Children and Youth (see Appendix B for a description of these resources and initiative). Excerpts of the Vanier Institute of the Family's article, with the Institute's permission, are provided below. All quotations are from *The Progress of Canada's Children 1996*, except where noted.

CANADA'S KIDS: THE FACTS
Canada's Kids: Who Do They Live With?
Good news
— "Nearly 80% of Canadian children, newborn to age 11, live with their biological parents."
— "Less than 1% live with teen mothers who usually have few financial resources."

Bad news
— "There is a significant minority of children and youth who are not growing up in their own families. These children are being raised in foster homes or group homes, some live in institutions for young offenders, while others are living on the street. While reliable estimates are hard to come by, child welfare experts estimate, for example, that there are 40,000 children and

youth in care at any one point in time in Canada. This does not include the children who cycle back and forth between the family and alternative care, which would bring the number closer to 100,000 per year."

— "Aboriginal children in particular are more likely to live in care than children in the general population — 4% compared to less than 1% in 1994."

Trends

— "Common law unions, lone-parent families and blended families are increasing."

— "Families are getting smaller and parents have children later in life."

— "Children make up a smaller proportion of our population."

— "Today, youth are more likely to remain at home longer than even a decade ago."

— "Changing immigration patterns mean that more Canadian children come from ethnically, racially and linguistically diverse backgrounds."

Canada's Kids: Are They Healthy and Safe?

Good news

— "The infant mortality rate has decreased by 75% over the past 30 years."

— "Young teens in Canada are among the most physically active of teens in 24 countries."

— "Teen pregnancies are declining as more teens use contraceptives. In 1992, 41.6 of every 1,000 young women became pregnant, less than half the American rate."

— "Between 1974 and 1992, the concentration of hazardous air toxins declined."

— "Injury-related deaths for children under 19 years of age dropped to 20 per 100,000 between 1981 and 1991."

— "More than 55% of children aged 0 to 11 years live with parents who report never using physical punishment."

— "The violent crime rate — an important barometer of public safety — dropped 4% between 1994 and 1995."

— "In 1994, children under 12 accounted for 6% of all crime victims, although they make up 16% of the population."

Bad news
— "The teen suicide rate has increased dramatically over the past 30 years, especially among teenage boys. Suicide is now the second leading cause of death — 13 per 100,000 teens."

— "In 1994, 5.7% of babies were born at a low birth weight."

— "One in four pregnant women smokes."

— "Nearly 40% of children under age 6 live in a home where one or more persons smoke regularly."

— "In comparison to other countries, a high percentage of young Canadian teens (10%) claim to be regular smokers."

— "Despite progress in reducing childhood injuries, the death rate for Canadian children aged 5 to 14 ranked 16th for boys and 15th for girls among 32 countries surveyed."

— "Youth between the ages of 12 and 19 — who make up 11% of the population — accounted for 20% of victims of violent crimes reported to the police."

Canada's Kids: Are They Socially Well-Adjusted?
Good news
— "Physical aggression by boys and girls actually decreases as they grow older."

— "School-age children in Canada tend to have good relationships with family members and friends."

Bad news
— As they grew older, children used indirect aggression with increasing frequency. (Indirect aggression refers to manipulations by the child that are intended to harm or deprive another person, while evading direct confrontation. Examples include spreading gossip, excluding someone from a group, or setting up another child for punishment (from an article by Dr. Richard E. Tremblay and others in *Growing Up in Canada*).

— "The rate of violent offences committed by youth aged 12 to 17 years more than doubled between 1986 and 1992. Violent crime now makes up 19% of all crimes committed by youth. Most of these are committed by a small minority of teens, mostly boys."

— "Teens, particularly girls, are more likely to report feeling lonely, depressed or unhappy about their lives than younger children."

Observations

— At every age, boys were more physically aggressive than girls, while girls showed higher levels of indirect aggression than boys (from an article by Tremblay and others in *Growing Up in Canada*).

— "A Quebec study of 4,000 schoolchildren found that 14% of the boys and 5% of the girls from the poorest districts were violent, compared to 5% of boys and 1% of girls from the wealthiest areas."

Canada's Kids: How Are They Doing at School?

Good news

— "The majority of children aged 4 to 9 (88%) have a positive attitude about learning and they look forward to school."

— "The 1994 nation-wide reading and writing tests of 16-year-olds found that 72% read at high levels and could interpret, evaluate and explore complex and sophisticated texts. In addition, 80% of students demonstrated the ability to write well. Overall, girls did much better than boys."

— "Canada has one of the highest enrollments in post-secondary institutions among industrialized countries: 35% of 20- to 24-year-olds attend college or university."

Bad news

— "Funding for kindergarten programs is being cut across Canada. Fewer children have access to high-quality preschool programs."

Canada's Parents: How Are They Doing?

Good news

— "More than 95% of parents report having a moderate or high degree of

social support from family, friends and neighbours."
— "Over 90% of parents surveyed in the NLSCY had scores that indicated good family relationships."
— "Most parents report positive interactions with their children."
— "Less than 10% of children up to the age of 11 lived with parents who were experiencing symptoms of depression in 1994."

Time crunch
— Parents "are having difficulty balancing work and family responsibilities: 50% of working mothers and 35% of working fathers report having difficulty managing their family time."
— In a decade, "parents in two-parent families with children under 18 have increased their combined weeks of employment by an average of 5.7 weeks — from 72.6 weeks a year in 1984, to 78.3 weeks in 1994."

Money crunch
— "Economic security has eroded among poor- and middle-income families."
— "The average after-tax income of families with children dropped between 1984 and 1994 — from $43,800 to $43,700."
— "The income gap is growing" between Canada's wealthiest and poorest parents.
— "The cost of raising children is the greatest expense that most Canadian families face — an estimated $150,000 to raise a child from birth to 18 years, including the cost of child care."
— "In 1994, 12% of families had at least one parent unemployed for more than six months."

Canada's Kids: The Issues
One out of five children lives in poverty
— "Even with government assistance, many children in Canada are poor. In 1994, one in five children under 18 years lived in families with incomes below Statistics Canada's low income cut-offs, including many whose families had incomes far below this poverty line. In fact, the average income of

poor families with children was $8,300 below the poverty line. Another 220,000 children lived in families with incomes within 10% of the poverty line. (In 1994, the Statistics Canada low income cut-off for a family of four in a large urban centre was $22,039.)"

Most poor kids live with two parents, but a disproportionately high number of Canada's poorest children are found in one-parent households.

More kids live with one parent
— "In 1995, there were over 1.1 million lone-parent families, an increase of 60% from 1981. In the past, most lone-parent families were created when one parent died. Today, divorce and separation are the major causes of lone parenthood."

— "Today, 86% of lone-parent families are headed by women, and these families are far more likely to experience poverty than those headed by men — 56% compared to 33%. The reason is twofold. Women who are employed generally receive lower wages than men, while unemployed women, primarily single mothers with young children, must rely on income security programs such as social assistance that set benefit rates below the poverty line."

Aboriginal children suffer more because of poor social conditions
— In 1991, more than 8% of the total Aboriginal population reported food shortages.

— The accurate poverty rate for Aboriginal children is unknown. We do know, however, that a very high proportion of Aboriginal peoples live below the poverty line, and many experience conditions similar to Third World countries.

— The infant death rate for Indian babies is almost twice the rate of non-Aboriginal infants.

— Compared to the total number of children in Canada, Indian children have a much higher death rate due to injuries. The injury rate is over 3 times greater for Indian teenagers than for non-Aboriginal youth.

— The suicide rate among Indian youth is 5 times that of the Canadian population as a whole (The Canadian Institute of Child Health. *The Health of Canada's Children: A CICH Profile*, 1994A).

More kids live with complex, changing relationships

— "Many children witness the separation of their parents, and these separations are occurring earlier in the child's life."

— "Approximately 8% of Canadian children born in the early 1960s experienced their parents' separation by the time they were six years old. In contrast, 18% of children born in the early 1980s saw their parents separate by age six."

— "In the past 20 years, the number of young children affected by a marital break-up has tripled."

Appendix B
HELPING CANADA KEEP SCORE

This appendix describes four ongoing initiatives designed to help analyse and evaluate how well children are doing in Canada: The National Longitudinal Survey of Children and Youth, *The Progress of Canada's Children*, the Community Social Reporting Project and the Better Beginnings, Better Futures Project.

The National Longitudinal Survey of Children and Youth (NLSCY) is a long-term study conducted in partnership by two federal departments: Human Resources Development Canada and Statistics Canada. The primary objective of the survey is to monitor the development and well-being of Canada's children as they grow from infancy to adulthood. More specifically, its objectives are:

— to determine the prevalence of various, biological, social and economic characteristics and risk factors among children and youth;

— to support Canadian understanding of the determinants of child development and well-being, and of the pathways of their influence on child outcomes; and

— to provide this information to policy and program officials for use in developing effective strategies to help young people.

Design: The survey is designed to follow a representative sample of Canadian children (22,831 children), aged newborn to 11 years. The progress of the children is tracked from the time the survey started on into their adulthood. Data collection occurs every two years: the first collection of information (cycle 1) took place in the winter of 1994-95; the second data collection (cycle 2) was completed in the summer of 1997.

Content: The survey examines a variety of factors thought to influence child growth and development. Data are collected on the child's parent(s) and other family members, on the characteristics of the child's family, on the neighbourhood in which the child lives and on the child's school. In addition, the survey collects data on the child's health, development, temperament, behaviour, relationships, child care and school experiences, participation in activities, and family and custody history.

Cycle 1 Research Program: In November 1996, the federal government published a volume entitled *Growing Up in Canada*, which presents the first research studies undertaken using the survey data. *Growing Up in Canada* includes articles by some of Canada's leading experts in child development. The articles deal with topics such as infant health; mathematics achievement in Grades 2 through 6, the characteristics and functioning of step-families, parenting practices, and emotional and behavioural problems in young children.

Around the time of the release of *Our Promise to Children*, the government will begin publishing further expert analysis related to cycle 1 data. Major areas of this research include:

CLASS INCOME AND CHILD OUTCOMES

DETERMINANTS OF CHILD DEVELOPMENT

CHILD DEVELOPMENT OUTCOMES

VULNERABLE POPULATIONS

"This ambitious study [the NLSCY], launched by the federal government, takes us a giant step further in our ability to understand child development. The NLSCY provides a unique opportunity to study the progress of children from infancy to adulthood. The results of this survey, once it has been operational for several years, hold great promise for sorting out the processes at work in ... child development."

Ross, Scott & Kelly (1996), pp. 15-45.

The Progress of Canada's Children, by the Canadian Council on Social Development, is an annual progress report pulling together information on many different aspects of child and family well-being. It is conducted by the Centre for International Statistics at the Canadian Council on Social Development with the support of the Laidlaw Foundation. The progress report will measure changes in children and family well-being over time.

The Progress of Canada's Children tracks both environmental indicators which influence child development and progression indicators which describe children's well-being over time. The environmental indicators include economic security, family care, physical safety, community resources and civic vitality. The progression indicators include health status, social engagement, academic performance and skill development which are organized by age groups. The primary source of information for the report comes from the data collected by the NLSCY.

A 50-page report is being published each year in a magazine format including photographs and graphics, similar to that used by the UNICEF publication, *The Progress of Nations*.

The Council hopes its annual report will challenge Canadians to "reconsider our priorities and the impact of policies and programs on the well-being of our children and youth. We believe that every child deserves an equal chance to develop to his or her potential and that our future depends on the ability of our young people to meet the demands of a complex society and a volatile economy."

The **Community Social Reporting Project** at the Centre for Studies of Children at Risk in Hamilton, Ontario is a three-year project funded by the Atkinson Charitable Foundation. The objective of this project is to develop, implement and test a self-sustaining, regular community-based system that will monitor the health and well-being of children and youth in a community. The system will initially be tested in two small- to mid-sized municipalities.

The general purpose of this kind of reporting is to provide particular community-specific information to help communities address identified areas of deficits and build on identified areas of strengths.

The Community Social Reporting Project is concerned with doing four things:

— identifying and unlocking existing community data, so that the community can use these data to the fullest;

— modifying and expanding data collection in the existing information systems in the community;

— exploring the possibility of developing new information systems; and
— tracking and analysing how the information is used to help determine its effect in the communities, particularly on the health and well-being of children and youth.

The Community Social Reporting Project will be developing a "community kit" designed to provide communities with the necessary tools they need to set up a sustainable monitoring system.

The **Better Beginnings, Better Futures Project** in Ontario is funded by three provincial ministries (Community and Social Services, Education, and Health) as well as Heritage Canada. It is the first long-term prevention research/demonstration project of its kind in Canada. The projects focus on children up to the age of 8 years living in 8 low-income communities in Ontario. The communities are funded to provide services designed to meet local needs as defined by residents. Program activities vary from one site to another but often include home visiting, school and child care enrichment, parent/family support programs and community-focused programs.

The research component addresses three general questions. Is the Better Beginnings model effective? What structures and processes are associated with project results? Is the Better Beginnings model affordable?

~ Information is being collected on a wide range of child, family and community characteristics. A group of children and their families will be followed for 20 years to measure the long-term effects of the Better Beginnings programs.

~ Narrative descriptions of the structures, processes, activities and organization of the programs in each of the 8 communities are being compiled into public documents on specific topics such as resident participation and local decision-making structures.

~ All program sites are using a common accounting system to investigate the costs of the model from its initiation, throughout the program period and the longitudinal follow-up.

Appendix C
RELEVANT CANADIAN ORGANIZATIONS

T he national organizations listed below are among a number in Canada that provide assistance, publications and/or technical support to professionals and the general public concerned about the well-being of children and families. Please contact these organizations for more information about their mission and mandate or to receive a listing of their publications and services.

Caledon Institute of Social Policy
620 -1600 Scott Street
Ottawa, Ontario
K1Y 4N7
T: (613) 729-3340
F: (613) 729-3896

The Caledon Institute of Social Policy is a social policy think-tank established in 1992. The goals of the institute are to provide rigorous, high quality research and analysis; to inform and influence public opinion; to foster public discussion on poverty and social policy; and to develop and promote concrete, practical proposals for the reform of social programs and social benefits.

Campaign 2000
c/o Family Service Association
355 Church Street
Toronto, Ontario
M5B 128
T: (416) 595-9230, ext. 244
F: (416) 595-0242

Campaign 2000 is a national movement to build awareness and support for the 1989 all-party House of Commons resolution to eliminate child poverty. Campaign 2000 is non-partisan, urging all Canadian elected officials to keep their promises to our children. Since its launch in 1991, Campaign 2000 has released publications (including its annual report card) and organized events to aid public education and advocacy.

Canadian Association of Family Resource Programs
101-30 Rosemount Avenue
Ottawa, Ontario
K1Y 1P4
T: (613) 728-3307
F: (613) 729-5421

The Canadian Association of Family Resource Programs (FRPC) is a national organization whose mission is to promote the well-being of families by providing national leadership, consultation and resources to those who care for children and support families.

Canadian Child Care Federation
100-30 Rosemount Avenue
Ottawa, Ontario
K1Y 1P4
T: (613) 729-5289
F: (613) 729-3159

The Canadian Child Care Federation (CCCF) is a national non-profit organization working to improve the quality of child care for Canada's children through its membership base of child care providers, programs and affiliated provincial/territorial organizations across the country. CCCF plays a leadership role in research and policy development, provision of national information services and publications, and facilitating communications in the field.

Canadian Council on Social Development
441 MacLaren Street, 4th Floor
Ottawa, Ontario
K2P 2H3
T: (613) 236-8977
F: (613) 236-2750

The Canadian Council on Social Development (CCSD) is a voluntary, non-profit organization. Its mission is to develop and promote progressive social policies through research, consultation, public education and advocacy. Affiliated with the CCSD is the Centre for International Statistics, whose mandate is to collect, analyse and disseminate Canadian and international data on families and children.

Canadian Education Association
Suite 8-200, 252 Bloor Street West
Toronto, Ontario
M5S 1V5
T: (416) 924-7721
F: (416) 924-3188

The mission of the Canadian Education Association (CEA) is to promote the improvement of education. The association is a leader in the national dialogue on education. CEA provides individuals interested in education with opportunities to meet, learn and discuss questions of common interest. CEA publications deal with key issues, disseminate educational research and provide practical information.

Canadian Institute for Advanced Research
701-179 John Street
Toronto, Ontario
M5T 1X4
T: (416) 971-4251
F: (416) 971-6169

The primary objective of the Canadian Institute for Advanced Research (CIAR) is to network talented people across institutional, regional, cultural and political boundaries to work on problems and opportunities of scientific, economic and social importance. More than 150 CIAR Fellows, Scholars and Associates from Canada and around the world conduct research in 8 program areas, including population health, human development and economic growth.

Canadian Institute of Child Health
512-885 Meadowlands Drive
Ottawa, Ontario
K2C 3N2
T: (613) 224-4144
F: (613) 224-4145

The mission of the Canadian Institute of Child Health (CICH) is to promote the health and well-being of and prevent illness in all children and youth. CICH achievements address the prevention of developmental disabilities, low birth weight, prematurity, child sexual abuse, and the monitoring of child health, environmental safety and breastfeeding.

Canadian Policy Research Networks
430-250 Albert Street
Ottawa, Ontario
K1P 6M1
T: (613) 567-7500
F: (613) 567-7640

The Canadian Policy Research Networks (CPRN) is a "virtual" institute — a non-profit research organization coordinated from Ottawa. It has organized three networks of researchers focused on work, health and family. The mission of CPRN is to create knowledge and lead debate on social and economic issues important to the well-being of Canadians to help build a more just and caring society.

Canadian Teachers' Federation
110 Argyle Avenue
Ottawa, Ontario
K2P 1B4
T: (613) 232-1505
F: (613) 232-1886

The Canadian Teachers' Federation (CTF) is the national voice for teachers in promoting high quality in education, the status of teachers and equity of opportunity through public education. CTF coordinates and facilitates the sharing of ideas, knowledge and skills among its 13 provincial/territorial member organizations which collectively represent more than 240,000 teachers. CTF's publications and resources are available to the general public.

Centre for Studies of Children at Risk
Faculty of Health Sciences
McMaster University and Children's Hospital at Chedoke-McMaster
Patterson Building
1200 Main Street West
Hamilton, Ontario
L8N 3Z5
T: (905) 521-2100, ext. 4348
F: (905) 574-6665

The Centre for Studies of Children at Risk (CSCR) was founded in 1992 with the co-sponsorship of Chedoke-McMaster Hospitals and McMaster University. It is an international centre of excellence dedicated to reducing the suffering caused by children's mental health problems and improving the quality of life for children all across Canada. CSCR focuses on a threefold mandate: scientific research, policy consultation and training.

Child Care Advocacy Association of Canada

323 Chapel Street
Ottawa, Ontario
K1N 7Z2
T: (613) 594-3196
F: (613) 594-9375

The Child Care Advocacy Association advocates for comprehensive, high-quality and non-profit child care programs. The organization provides focus and leadership to social policy activists, labour groups, women's organizations and the child care community through ongoing campaigns designed to improve the accessibility, availability and quality of child care services across the country.

Child Welfare League of Canada

312-180 Argyle Avenue
Ottawa, Ontario
K2P 1B7
T: (613) 235-4412
F: (613) 788-5075

The Child Welfare League of Canada (CWLC) is dedicated to protecting and promoting the well-being of Canada's children, particularly those who are at risk because of poverty, abuse and neglect. CWLC's 71 member agencies serve approximately 50,000 children in care and provide family preservation, prevention and protection services to more than 500,000 children and their families.

Family Service Canada

600-220 Laurier Avenue West
Ottawa, Ontario
K1P 5Z9
T: (613) 230-9960
F: (613) 230-5884

Family Service Canada (FSC) is a national organization representing the concerns of families and family-serving agencies across Canada. Through public awareness initiatives, leadership training and quality assurance programs, public policy development and networking, the organization promotes investment in family well-being.

National Crime Prevention Council
130 Albert Street
Ottawa, Ontario
K1A 0H8
T: (613) 941-0505
F: (613) 952-3515

The National Crime Prevention Council is an independent, voluntary council whose mission is to develop strategies to empower individuals and their communities to improve their safety, security and well-being. Working with partners throughout the country, the council is finding new ways to influence the development of policy and programs which will help Canadian children and youth grow up in safe and nurturing environments.

The Vanier Institute of the Family
94 Centrepoint Drive
Nepean, Ontario
K2G 6B1
T: (613) 228-8500
F: (613) 228-8007

The Vanier Institute of the Family is a national voluntary organization dedicated to promoting the well-being of Canada's families through research, publications, public education and advocacy. Through its publications and other activities, the institute maintains regular contact with some 6,000 individuals, organizations and representatives from the public and private sectors.

Voices for Children
1200-415 Yonge Street
Toronto, Ontario
M5B 2E7
T: (416) 408-2121, ext. 269
F: (416) 408-2122

Voices for Children is a coalition of organizations from many different sectors — from health and education to business and labour. Through a comprehensive public education campaign, Voices for Children is building a movement to change public attitudes and commitment to the well-being of all children and youth in our society. Voices for Children believes that everyone can make a difference for children; their social and economic well-being is important to us all.

Appendix D
HEALTH CANADA'S GOALS FOR HEALTHY CHILD AND YOUTH DEVELOPMENT

MISSION
To safeguard and improve the health and well-being of all children and youth in Canada.

GOALS
Value all children and youth in Canada and share responsibility for their healthy development.

Support families in their role as the primary caregivers of children.

Make health promotion and prevention of disease, disability and injury among children and youth a priority of healthy public policies.

Reduce child and family poverty.

Protect children and youth from abuse, violence, inequity and discrimination.

Ensure that young people have opportunities to participate in decisions about their healthy development and encourage them to make healthy life choices.

Strengthen the capacity of communities to promote and improve healthy child and youth development.

Develop collaborative, cost-effective strategies to achieve measurable improvements in health outcomes for children and youth.

Appendix E
CRITERIA FOR RESEARCH INCLUDED IN
OUR PROMISE TO CHILDREN

~ Research that is methodically sound. When child outcomes are compared, children/families are from similar backgrounds or statistical procedures are used to control differences.

~ Where research suggests a possible relationship which has not yet been established, it is represented as informed opinion, not research evidence.

~ Whenever possible, Canadian examples are used. International examples are used where relevant findings appear to be transferable to Canadian environments and are able to fill gaps in Canadian research.

~ Research findings include research reports and surveys. More subjective material, such as focus group summaries, opinion polls or personal interviews with individuals, are presented as such.

~ Much of the research was collected from existing reviews on the determinants of healthy child development.

Appendix F
SPONSORS, ADVISORS, FUNDERS AND CONTRIBUTORS

SPONSORS OF *OUR PROMISE TO CHILDREN*

The Founders' Network of the Canadian Institute for Advanced Research

The Founders' Network consists of individuals across Canada and in other countries who contributed to the founding and the first 14 years of development of the Canadian Institute for Advanced Research. The Founders' Network builds linkages among this diverse group of individuals from the academic, private and public sectors, based on their interest in the continuing application of knowledge gained from the work of the Institute. One particular area of focus is the relationship among the new concepts of economic growth and social change and the determinants of health and human development, particularly as they relate to early childhood.

Centre for Studies of Children at Risk

The Centre for Studies of Children at Risk (CSCR) was founded in 1992 with the co-sponsorship of the Chedoke-McMaster Hospitals and McMaster University. It is an international centre of excellence dedicated to reducing the burden of suffering caused by children's mental health problems and improving the quality of life for children all across Canada.

In order to treat and prevent destructive emotional and behavioural problems in children, sound, measurable research is vital. CSCR focuses on using this information to aid in the development of:
~ cost-effective ways of interrupting development of these problems in children;
~ responsible public policy to improve children's mental health; and
~ community-based teaching to train professionals and educate the public about children's mental health.

The Centre is bridging the gap between what researchers know and what agencies and communities actually do.

FUNDERS OF *OUR PROMISE TO CHILDREN*

The Childhood and Youth Division of Health Canada

The Childhood and Youth Division of Health Canada serves as a centre of expertise, leadership and coordination within the federal government and Health Canada for issues, activities and programs concerning children and youth. It is a focal point for policy development, research and strategic analysis of trends regarding children and youth.

Invest in Kids Foundation

Invest in Kids Foundation is a national organization, founded in 1994, dedicated to ensuring Canada's children have the opportunity to grow into caring, competent and resilient adults. The Foundation directs its efforts in three key areas:

~ Proven early intervention programs for children aged 0-5, who are most at risk for abuse and developmental compromise, and their families.

~ Proven early assessment programs to identify physical, emotional, social and developmental problems in young children.

~ Public awareness and educational initiatives designed to communicate the importance of early child development and parenting.

The efforts of the Invest in Kids Foundation focus on children from infancy to five years of age, the most critical period of development. The Foundation promotes best practices for prevention and early intervention, and identifies and replicates proven and effective programs. The Board of Advisors for Invest in Kids Foundation is comprised of experts in the field of child development.

Imperial Oil Charitable Foundation

Children are at the heart of the Imperial Oil Charitable Foundation's giving. The Foundation has made a commitment to support various organizations that make a difference for kids through sports, health, education and culture. The Esso Kids Program is the umbrella under which Imperial Oil manages its involvement with children's charities and organizations. Approximately two-thirds of the company's annual contributions are allocated to child and youth-centred causes.

Supporting programs that create and foster healthier lifestyles for children through the Esso Kids Program is regarded by the company as an investment in the future of Canada. It is also viewed as one of the most meaningful and effective ways that Imperial Oil can make a difference in the communities in which they live and operate.

The Department of Justice

The responsibilities of the Department of Justice toward children and youth are several, arising from their general responsibility for criminal law, as well as for marriage and divorce. The Department is responsible for policy and law reform on youth justice, carried out in close cooperation with the provinces which are responsible for the administration of the justice system. The Department of Justice is also a partner in the federal government family violence initiative, and seeks to address this problem through legislative reform, research, funding for community-based projects, and public legal education projects.

Placing an emphasis on the victimization of children, the Department seeks to ensure adequate protection for children in our criminal law. Responsibility for the Divorce Act includes the development of child-centred policies in such areas as child support and custody. Several other broad departmental initiatives recognize the need to give priority for children and youth, including the Aboriginal Justice and Crime Prevention initiatives, as well as much of the Department's international public law work.

Advisory Committee Members
Our Promise to Children

Dr. Dan Offord, Chair
Director, Centre for Studies of
Children at Risk (CSCR)
Hamilton, Ontario

Senator Landon Pearson
Senate of Canada
Ottawa, Ontario

Ms. Carolyn Harrison
Acting Manager
Family and Child Health Unit
Health Canada
Ottawa, Ontario

Professor Camil Bouchard
Director, LAREHS
University of Quebec at Montreal
Montreal, Quebec

Dr. Paul Steinhauer
Department of Psychiatry
The Hospital for Sick Children
Toronto, Ontario

Mr. Robert Glossop
Executive Director
Vanier Institute of the Family
Nepean, Ontario

Dr. J. Fraser Mustard
Principal Advisor
Founders' Network
Canadian Institute for Advanced
Research
Toronto, Ontario

Mr. Brian Ward
Director
Childhood and Youth Division
Health Canada
Ottawa, Ontario

Ms. Jane Fitzgerald
Administrator
Family and Children's Services
Department of Community Services
Halifax, Nova Scotia

Dr. David Ross
Executive Director
Canadian Council on Social
Development
Ottawa, Ontario

Ms. Katherine Scott
Senior Research and Policy
Associate
Canadian Council on Social
Development
Ottawa, Ontario

Dr. Denise Avard
Executive Director
Canadian Institute of Child Health
Ottawa, Ontario

Dr. Freda Martin
Executive Director
Hincks Centre for Children and
Adolescents
Toronto, Ontario

Dr. Clyde Hertzman
Department of Health Care and
Epidemiology
University of British Columbia
Vancouver, British Columbia

Ms. Kathleen Guy
Project Director
Ottawa, Ontario

INDIVIDUALS INTERVIEWED FOR *OUR PROMISE TO CHILDREN*

Denise Avard, Executive Director, Canadian Institute of Child Health, Ottawa, Ontario

Camil Bouchard, Director, LAREHS, University of Quebec at Montreal, Montreal, Quebec

Claire Chamberland, Professor, University of Quebec at Montreal, Montreal, Quebec

Rick Ferron, Principal, Sunset Park Public School, North Bay, Ontario

Don Fuchs, Dean, Faculty of Social Work, University of Manitoba, Winnipeg, Manitoba

David Hall, Manager, Dufferin Mall, Toronto, Ontario

Clyde Hertzman, Department of Health Care and Epidemiology, University of British Columbia, Vancouver, British Columbia

Susan Jewkes, Previous Co-ordinator, Adolescent Health Project, Antigonish, Nova Scotia

Beverley Kirby, Director, Port au Port Community Education Initiative, Port au Port, Newfoundland

Freda Martin, Executive Director, Hincks Centre for Children and Adolescents, Toronto, Ontario

Fraser Mustard, Founders' Network of the Canadian Institute for Advanced Research, Toronto, Ontario

Marvyn Novick, School of Social Work, Ryerson Polytechnic University, Toronto, Ontario

Dan Offord, Director, Centre for Studies of Children at Risk, Hamilton, Ontario

Holly Paxton, Neighbourhood Assistant, Sir William MacDonald Elementary School, Vancouver, British Columbia

Charlotte Rosenbaum, Executive Director, North Kingston Community Health Centre, Kingston, Ontario

Paul Steinhauer, Voices for Children, and The Hospital for Sick Children, Toronto, Ontario

John Stephens, Vice-Principal, Sunset Park Public School, North Bay, Ontario

Richard Tremblay, Department of Psychology, University of Montreal, Montreal, Quebec

Debbie Wintle, Counsellor, Sunset Park Public School, North Bay, Ontario

ADDITIONAL INDIVIDUALS CONTRIBUTING RESEARCH ADVICE AND ASSISTANCE

Maureen Baker, School of Social Work, McGill University, Montreal, Quebec

Dawn Blessing, Site Researcher, North Kingston Better Beginnings, Kingston, Ontario

Rob Brown, Research Department, Toronto Board of Education, Toronto, Ontario

Robbie Case, Institute of Child Study at the University of Toronto, Toronto, Ontario

Edith Doucet, Director, Office of Childhood Services, Saint John, New Brunswick

Jane Fitzgerald, Administrator, Family and Children's Services, Nova Scotia Department of Community Services, Halifax, Nova Scotia

David Foot, Economics Department, University of Toronto, Toronto, Ontario

Margo Craig Garrison, Previous Acting Director, Family & Child Health Unit, Health Canada, Ottawa, Ontario

Bob Glossop, Executive Director, Vanier Institute of the Family, Nepean, Ontario

Carolyn Gorlick, School of Social Work, King's College, University of Western Ontario

Dan Keating, Ontario Institute for Studies in Education at the University of Toronto, Toronto, Ontario

Judith Maxwell, President, Canadian Policy Research Networks, Ottawa, Ontario

Heather Munro-Blum, Vice-President, Research, University of Toronto, Toronto, Ontario

Charles Pascal, Executive Director, Atkinson Charitable Foundation, Toronto, Ontario

Senator Landon Pearson, Senate of Canada, Ottawa, Ontario

Allan Pence, School of Child and Youth Care, University of Victoria, Victoria, British Columbia

Ray Peters, Research Director, Better Beginnings, Better Futures, Queen's University

Suzanne Peters, Director, Family Network, Canadian Policy Research Networks, Ottawa, Ontario

David Ross, Executive Director, Canadian Council on Social Development, Ottawa, Ontario

Carol Crill Russell, Senior Researcher & Policy Analyst, Ontario Ministry of Community & Social Services, Toronto, Ontario

Marlene Scardamalia, Ontario Institute for Studies in Education at the University of Toronto, Toronto, Ontario

Katherine Scott, Senior Research and Policy Associate, Canadian Council on Social Development, Ottawa, Ontario

Craig Shields, Laidlaw Foundation, Toronto, Ontario

J. Doug Willms, Atlantic Centre for Policy Research in Education, Faculty of Education, University of New Brunswick

INDIVIDUALS CONTRIBUTING TO THE DEVELOPMENT OF THE MANUSCRIPT

Jane Bertrand • Clyde Graham • Cheryl Hamilton • Anne Holloway • Carol Kushner • Heather Lang-Runtz • Ernest Loevinsohn • David Newing • Ann Silversides • Judith Whitehead • members of the book's advisory committee

Bibliography

Ainslie, R.C. & Anderson, C.W. (1984) "Day Care: Children's Relationships to Their Mothers and Caregivers: An Inquiry into the Conditions for the Development of Attachment." R.C. Ainslie (ed). *The Child and the Day Care Setting: Qualitative Variations and Development.* New York: Praeger. p. 98-132

Ainsworth, M. & Marvin, R. (1995) "On the Shaping of Attachment Theory and Research: An Interview with Mary D.S. Ainsworth." *Caregiving, Cultural, and Cognitive Perspectives on Secure-Base Behavior and Working Models: New Growing Points of Attachment Theory and Research.* E. Waters, B. Vaughn, G. Posada, & K. Kondo-Ikemura (eds). Monographs of the Society for Research in Child Development. (Serial No. 244, Vol. 60, Nos. 2-3, 1995). p. 3-24

Andres, J., Stroud, C., Moore, T., & Peplar, D. (1996) *Babies Best Start Interim Evaluation Report August 1996.* Scarborough: Babies Best Start

Antigonish Adolescent Health Survey (1991) *The Voice of Teens.* Antigonish

Bagley C. & Tremblay, P. (In press) "Suicidality Problems of Gay and Bisexual Males: Evidence from a Random Community Survey of 750 Men Aged 18 to 27" in C. Bagley & R. Ramsey (eds), *Suicidal Behaviors in Adolescent and Adults: Taxonomy, Understanding and Prevention.* Brookfield, Vermont: Avebury

Bandura, A., Barbaranelli, C., Caprara, G.V., & Pastorelli, C. (1996) "Multifaceted Impact of Self-Efficacy Beliefs on Academic Functioning. *Child Development,* 67, 1206-1222

Beckwith, L. (1990) "Adaptive and Maladaptive Parenting — Implications for Prevention" in S. Meisels & J. Shonkoff (eds), *Handbook of Early Childhood Intervention.* New York: Cambridge University Press. p. 53-77

Beland, C. (1996) "Employers and Family Security." *Family Security in Insecure Times*. Vol. II, Perspectives. Ottawa: National Forum on Family Security, Canadian Council on Social Development

Berk, I. (1997) *Child Development*, 4th ed. Needham Heights, Mass.: Allyn and Bacon

Berk, I. (1994) "Vygotsky's Theory: The Importance of Make-Believe Play." *Young Children*, November. p. 30-39

Bouchard, C. (1987) *Child Maltreatment in Montreal*, Montreal: University of Quebec

Bronfenbrenner, U. (1979) *The Ecology of Human Development: Experiments by Nature and Design*. Cambridge, Massachusetts: Harvard University Press

Brown, J.L. & Pollitt, E. (1996) "Malnutrition, Poverty & Intellectual Development." *Scientific American*, February

Campbell, F.A. & Ramey, C.T. (1994) "Effects of Early Intervention on Intellectual and Academic Achievement: A Follow-up Study of Children from Low-income Families." *Child Development*, 65, 684-698

Canadian Council on Social Development (1996) *The Progress of Canada's Children 1996*. Ottawa

Canadian Institute of Child Health (1994A) *The Health of Canada's Children: A CICH Profile*, 2nd edition. Ottawa

Canadian Institute of Child Health (1994B) *Child Sexual Abuse Prevention: A Resource Kit*. Ottawa

Carignan, P. (1992) *Parents and Children, Winners: 5 Promotion and Prevention Projects*. Montreal: Childhood-Family-Community, Developing Networks

Carnegie Corporation of New York (1994) *Starting Points: Meeting the Needs of Our Youngest Children*. New York

Case, R. (1997) *Socioeconomic Gradients in Mathematical Ability and Their Responsiveness to Intervention during Early Childhood. Working Paper CIAR Human Development.* Toronto: Canadian Institute of Advanced Research

Coles, R. (1997) *The Moral Intelligence of Children.* New York: Random House

Coles, R. (1990) *The Spiritual Lives of Children.* Boston: Houghton Mifflin

Cunningham, C., Cunningham, L., Martorelli, V., Tran, A., Young, J., & Zacharias, R. (1997) "The Effects of Primary Division, Student-Mediated Conflict Resolution Programs on Playground Aggression" submitted to *Journal of Child Psychology and Psychiatry*

Cyander, M. & Mustard, F. (1997) "Brain Development, Competence and Coping Skills" in *Entropy*: Founders' Network Report in support of the Canadian Institute for Advanced Research, Spring, Vol.1, Issue 1, 5-6

Derman-Sparks, L. & the A.B.C. Task Force (1989) *Anti-bias Curriculum: Tools for Empowering Young Children.* Washington, D.C.: National Association for the Education of Young Children

Desjardins, E. (1996) *Executive Summary and Introduction of Healthiest Babies Possible Report: Evaluation 1991-95.* Toronto: Toronto Public Health Department

DiFranza, J., & Lew, R. (1995) "Effect of Maternal Cigarette Smoking on Pregnancy Complications and Sudden Infant Death Syndrome." *The Journal of Family Practice*, Vol. 40 No. 4 (Apr.), 385-394

Doherty, G. (1997) *Zero to Six: The Basis for School Readiness*, R-97-8E. Ottawa: Applied Research Branch, Strategic Policy, Human Resources Development Canada

Doherty, G. (1996) *The Great Child Care Debate: The Long Term Effects of Non-Parental Child Care.* Occasional Paper No. 7. Toronto: Childcare Resource and Research Unit, University of Toronto

Doherty, G. (1992) *Addressing the Issue of Lack of Preschool Readiness in Preschoolers*. A paper prepared for the Prosperity Steering Committee, Canada

Doherty-Derkowski, G. (1995) *Quality Matters: Excellence in Early Childhood Programs*. Don Mills: Addison-Wesley

Duxbury, L. & Higgins, C. (1994) "Families in the Economy" in M. Baker (ed), *Canada's Changing Families: Challenges to Public Policy*. Ottawa: The Vanier Institute of the Family

Dweck, C. & Leggett, E. (1988) "A Social-Cognitive Approach to Motivation and Personality." *Psychological Review*, 95, 256-273

Elicker, J. & Fortner-Wood, C. (1995) "Adult-Child Relationships in Early Childhood Programs." *Young Children* November, 69-78

Erikson, M.F., Sroufe, L.A., & Egeland, B. (1985) "The Relationship Between Quality of Attachment and Behavior Problems in Preschool in a High-Risk Sample" in I. Bretherton & E. Waters (eds), *Growing Points in Attachment Theory and Research*. Monographs of the Society for Research in Child Development 50 (1-2): Series No. 209. p. 147-166

Evans, J. (1996) "Reconstructing the Context for Child Development." Presentation at Canada's Children, Canada's Future Conference. November 25, 1996. Ottawa

Family & Work Institute (1997) *I am Your Child: The New Brain Research and Your Child's Healthy Development*. New York

Fanjoy, S. (1994) "Meadow Lake Tribal Council: Indian Child Care Program." Focus 2 on Child Care Initiatives Fund Projects. Ottawa: Canadian Child Care Federation

Ferris, C. (1996) "The Rage of Innocents: Windows on the Biology of Childhood Violence." *The Sciences*. March/April, 22-26

Fogel, R. (1994) *Economic Growth, Population Theory, and Physiology: The Bearing of Long-Term Processes in the Making of Economic Policy.* Working Paper No. 4638. Cambridge, Massachusetts: National Bureau of Economic Research

Fontaine, P. (1995) *Welcome and Blessing.* Presentation at the National Symposium on Community Action for Children. November 5. Winnipeg: Healthy Child Development Project

Frank, J. & Mustard, J.F. (1994) "The Determinants of Health from a Historical Perspective." Daedalus: Health and Wealth. *Journal of the American Academy of Arts and Sciences*, Fall, 1-20

Garbarino, J. (1995) *Raising Children in a Socially Toxic Environment.* San Francisco: Jossey-Bass

Garbarino, J. (1990) "The Human Ecology of Early Risk" in S. Meisels & J. Shonkoff (eds), *Handbook of Early Childhood Intervention.* New York: Cambridge University Press. p. 78-96

Garbarino, J. (1982) *Children and Families in the Social Environment.* Hawthorne, New York: Aldine Publishing

Glossop, R. (1996) Presentation at Canada's Children, Canada's Future Conference. November 25-27. Ottawa

Gorlick, C. (1995) *Taking Chances: Single Mothers and their Children Exiting Welfare.* London, Ontario: University of Western Ontario

Greene, B. & Wilbee, S. (1992) *Foetal Alcohol Syndrome: A Preventable Tragedy.* Report of the Standing Committee on Health and Welfare, Social Affairs, Seniors and the Status of Women. Ottawa: House of Commons Issue No. 10

Hanvey, L. (1993) "Working Paper on Health Status." *Working Papers on the Determinants of Healthy Child and Youth Development.* Toronto: Premier's Council on Health, Well-being and Social Justice

Health Canada (1996) *Turning Points*. Ottawa: Government of Canada

Health Canada (1993) *Kids Talk and Videotape*. Ottawa: Government of Canada

Healthy Child Development Project (1995) *Healthy Children, Healthy Communities: A Compendium of Approaches from Across Canada*. Ottawa

Healthy Child Development Project (1995) National Symposium on Community Action for Children. November 5-7. Winnipeg

Hertzman, C. & Mustard, F. (1997) "A Healthy Early Childhood = A Heathy Adult Life" in *Entropy*: Founders' Network Report in support of the Canadian Institute for Advanced Research, Spring, Vol.1, Issue 1, 3-4

Higgins, C., Duxbury, L. & Lee, C. (1993) *Balancing Work and Family: A Study of the Canadian Private Sector*. London: National Centre for Research, Management & Development, University of Western Ontario

Howes, C., Rodning, C., Galluzzo, D.C. & Myers, L. (1988) "Attachment and Child Care: Relationships with Mother and Caregiver." *Early Childhood Research Quarterly* 14(2), 140-151

Human Resources Development Canada & Statistics Canada (1997) *School Component*. Ottawa: Statistics Canada

Human Resources Development Canada & Statistics Canada (1996) *Growing Up in Canada: National Longitudinal Survey of Children and Youth*. Ottawa: Government of Canada

Insight Canada Research (1993) *Aspirations Report*. Toronto: Ontario Premier's Council on Health, Well-being and Social Justice

Johnston, Basil (1995) *The Manitous: The Spiritual World of the Ojibway*. Toronto: Key Porter Books Ltd

Kagan, J. (1994) *Galen's Prophecy: Temperament in Human Nature*. New York: HarperCollins

Keating, D. (1996) *Early Childhood Programs.* Presentation at the Symposium on National Projects for a New Canada. March 2. Toronto: Glendon Campus, York University

Keating, D. (1993) "Developmental Determinants of Health and Well-being." *Working Papers on the Determinants of Healthy Child and Youth Development.* Toronto: Ontario Premier's Council on Health, Well-being and Social Justice

Keating, D. (1992) *The Learning Society in the Information Age.* Human Development Working Paper No. 2. Toronto: Canadian Institute for Advanced Research

Keating, D. & Mustard, F. (1996) "The National Longitudinal Survey of Children and Youth: An Essential Element for Building a Learning Society in Canada" in *Growing Up in Canada: National Longitudinal Survey of Children and Youth.* Ottawa: Human Resources Development Canada & Statistics Canada. p. 7-13

Keating, D. & Mustard, F. (1993) "Social Economic Factors and Human Development" in D. Ross (ed), *Family Security in Insecure Times* Vol.1. Ottawa: National Forum on Family Security, Canadian Council on Social Development

King, A. & Peart, M.J. (1990) *The Good School.* Toronto: Ontario Teachers Federation

Kohlberg, L. (1969) "Stage and Sequence: The Cognitive-Developmental Approach to Socialization" in D.A. Goslin (ed), *Handbook of Socialization Theory and Research.* Chicago: Rand McNally. p. 347-480

Kuebli, J. (1994) "Young Children's Understanding of Everyday Emotions". *Young Children* March, 36-47

Landy, S. & Tam, K.K. (1996) "Yes, Parenting Does Make a Difference to the Development of Children in Canada" in *Growing Up in Canada: National Longitudinal Survey of Children and Youth*. Ottawa: Human Resources Development Canada & Statistics Canada. p. 103-118

Lazar, I. & Darlington, R. (1982) "Lasting Effects of Early Education: A Report from the Consortium for Longitudinal Studies." *Monographs of the Society for Research in Child Development* 47, 2-3

Lee, V., Brooks-Gunn, J., & Schnur, E. (1988) "How Does Head-Start Work? A 1-Year Follow-up Comparison of Disadvantaged Children Attending Head-Start, No Preschool and Other Preschool Programmes." *Developmental Psychology*, 24, 210-222

Logan, R. & Belliveau, J. (1995) "Working Mothers." *Canadian Social Trends*. Spring. Ottawa: Statistics Canada

Lowe, C.U. & Boone, M. (1992) "Poverty, Futures & Child Health" in W.J. Tze & R.J. Haggerty (eds), *Monograph: Child Health 2000: World Congress & Exposition on Child Health*. Vancouver: Child Health 2000

Lugtig, D. & Fuchs, D. (1992) *Building on the Strengths of Local Neighborhood: Social Network Ties for the Prevention of Child Maltreatment*. Final report of the Neighbourhood Parent Support Project. Winnipeg: Child and Family Service Research Group, Faculty of Social Work, University of Manitoba

MacMillan, H., Fleming, J., Trocme, N., Boyle, M., Wong, M., Racine, Y., Beardslee, W., & Offord, D. (1997) *Prevalence of Child Physical and Sexual Abuse in the Community: Results from the Ontario Health Supplement*. Hamilton: Centre for Studies of Children at Risk

Mainous, A. & Heuston, W. (1994) "The Effect of Smoking Cessation During Pregnancy on Preterm Delivery and Low Birthweight." *The Journal of Family Practice*, Vol. 38, No. 3, 262-266

Maloney, C. (1996) *How Does the Spiritual Reveal Itself in the Lives of Children?* (Unpublished manuscript). Toronto: Metropolitan Toronto Catholic Children's Aid

Maxwell, J. (1996) Presentation at National Conference of the Community Foundations of Canada. May 23-25. London, Ontario

McCreary Centre Society (1993) *Adolescent Health Survey: Province of British Columbia.* Vancouver

Meaney, M.J., Aitken, D.H., Van Berkel, C., Bhatnagar, S., & Sapolsky, R.M. (1988) "Effect of Neonatal Handling on Age-related Impairments Associated with Hippocampus." *Science* 239, 766-768

Morrison, J., Williams, G.M., Najman, J.M., Andersen, M.J., & Keeping, J.D. (1993) "Birthweight Below the Tenth Percentile: The Relative and Attributable Risks of Maternal Tobacco Consumption and Other Factors." *Environmental Health Perspectives Supplements* Vol. 101, 225-227

Muscati, S., Gray-Donald, K., & Newson, E. (1994) "Interaction of Smoking and Maternal Weight Status in Influencing Infant Size." *Canadian Journal of Public Health*, Vol 85, No. 6, 407-412

Mustard, F. (1996) "Technology, Information and the Evolution of Social Policy: The Chips for Neurons Revolution and Socio-Economic Change" in Courchene, T.J. (ed), *Policy Frameworks for a Knowledge Economy.* Bell Canada Papers on Economic and Public Policy. Kingston: John Deutsch Institute for the Study of Economic Policy

Mustard, C. (1993) The Utilization of Prenatal Care and Relationship to Birth Weight Outcome in Winnipeg 1987-88. Winnipeg: Manitoba Centre for Health Policy and Education

Myers, D. (1996) *Exploring Psychology*, 3rd ed. New York: Worth Publishers

Nash, J.M. (1997) "Fertile Minds." *Time.* Canadian edition, June 9. p. 46-54

National Crime Prevention Council (1997) *The Dollars and Sense of a Comprehensive Crime Prevention Strategy for Canada.* Ottawa

National Crime Prevention Council (1996) *Preventing Crime by Investing in Families: An Integrated Approach to Promote Positive Outcomes in Children.* Ottawa

Nechenechea Dakwa ul (1995) Community Poster Session Presentation at the National Symposium on Community Action for Children. November 5-7. Winnipeg.

Newsweek (1997) "Your Child: From Birth to Three." Special edition, Spring/Summer

Normand, C., Zoccolillo, M., Tremblay, R., McIntyre, L., Boulerice, B., McDuff, P., Perusse, D., & Barr, R. (1996) "In the Beginning: Looking for the Roots of Babies' Difficult Temperament" in *Growing Up in Canada: National Longitudinal Survey of Children and Youth.* Ottawa: Human Resources Development Canada & Statistics Canada. p. 57-68

Office of Health Promotion, B.C. Ministry of Health & Ministry Responsible for Seniors (1991) *Healthy Schools — A Resource Guide for Teachers.* Government of British Columbia

Offord, D., Boyle, M.H., Szatmari, P., Rae-Grant, N.I., Links, P.S., Cadman, D.T., Byles, J.A., Crawford, J.W., Munroe-Blum, H., Bryne, C., Thomas, H., & Woodward, C.A. (1987) "Ontario Child Health Study." *Archives of General Psychiatry*, 44, 832-836

Offord, D. & Jones, M.B. (1991) *The Ottawa Project: A Compensatory Recreation and Skill-development Program.* Presented at the Annual Meeting, American Association for the Advancement of Science. February 14-29. Washington, DC

Offord, D. & Lipman, E. (1996) "Emotional and Behavioral Problems" in *Growing Up in Canada: National Longitudinal Survey of Children and Youth.* Ottawa: Human Resources Development Canada & Statistics Canada. p. 119-126

Offord, D. (In press) "Bridging Development, Prevention and Policy" in D. Stoff, J. Brieling, & J.D. Maser (eds), *Handbook of Antisocial Behaviour*. New York: John Wiley & Sons

Ontario Coalition for Children and Youth (1994) *Young Voices: Final Report*. Toronto: Premier's Council on Health, Well-being and Social Justice

Organization for Economic Co-operation and Development (1995) *Economic Surveys Canada*. Paris

Organization for Economic Co-operation and Development & Statistics Canada (1995) *Literacy, Economy and Society: Results of the First International Adult Literacy Survey*. Paris: Organization for Economic Co-operation and Development, and Ottawa: Minister of Industry Canada

Perry, B. (1997) *The Mismatch Between Opportunity and Investment*. Houston: CIVITAS Child Trauma Programs (and) Chicago: CIVITAS Initiative

Perry, B. (1995) "Incubated in Terror: Neurodevelopmental Factors in the Cycle of Violence" in J. Osofsky (ed), *Children, Youth and Violence: Searching for Solutions*. New York: The Guilford Press

Peters, S. (1995) *Exploring Canadian Values: Foundations for Well-Being*. Ottawa: Canadian Policy Research Networks

Peters, R. DeV. & Russell, C. (1996) "Promoting Development and Preventing Disorder: The Better Beginnings, Better Futures Project." In R. DeV. Peters & R.J. McMahon (eds), *Preventing Childhood Disorders, Substance Abuse and Delinquency*. Thousand Oaks, California: Sage, p. 19-47

Picot, G. & Myles, J. (1996) *Social Transfers, Changing Family Structure and Low Income Among Children*. Ottawa: Statistics Canada, Analytical Studies Branch, No. 82

Pointe-Calumet (1995) Community Poster Session Presentation at the National Symposium on Community Action for Children. November 5-7. Winnipeg

Putnam, R. (1993) *Making Democracy Work*. Princeton, New York: Princeton University Press

Quebec Ministry of Health & Social Services (1991) *Quebec: Crazy About Our Kids*. Government of Quebec

Rosenberg, N. & Birdzell, L.E. (1986) *How the West Grew Rich*. New York: Basic Books

Ross, D., Scott, K., & Kelly, M. (1996) "Overview: Children in Canada in the 1990s" in *Growing Up in Canada: National Longitudinal Survey of Children and Youth*. Ottawa: Human Resources Development Canada & Statistics Canada. p. 15-45

Royal Commission on Aboriginal Peoples (1995) *Choosing Life: Special Report on Suicide Among Aboriginal People*. Ottawa: Canada Communications Group

Rubenstein, J. & Howes, C. (1979) "Caregiver and Infant Behavior in Day Care and in Homes." *Developmental Psychology*, Vol. 15, No. 1, 1-24

Rutter, M. (1979) "Protective Factors in Children's Response to Stress and Disadvantage" in M.W. Kenet & J. Rolf (eds), *Primary Prevention of Psychopathology, Social Competence in Children* (Vol. III). Hanover, New Hampshire: University Press of New England. p. 49-74

Rutter, M. (1985) "Family and School Influences on Cognitive Development." *Journal of Child Psychology* 26, 683-700

Rutter, M. & Rutter, M. (1993) *Developing Minds: Challenge and Continuity Across the Life Span*. London, England: Penguin Books

Schweinhart, L.J., Barnes, H.V., & Weikart, D.P. (1993) *Significant Benefits: The High/Scope Perry Preschool Study Through Age 27*. Monographs of 10 High/Scope Educational Research Foundation, 10. Ypsilanti, Michigan: High/Scope Press

Shields, C. (1993) *Community Systems Initiative: An Introductory Overview.* Toronto: Laidlaw Foundation

Shore, R. (1997) *Rethinking the Brain: New Insights into Early Development.* New York: Family and Work Institute

Silva-Wayne, S. (1995) "Contributions to Resilience in Children and Youth: What Successful Child Welfare Graduates Say" in J. Hudson & B. Galaway (eds), *Child Welfare in Canada Research and Policy Implications.* Toronto: Thompson Educational Publishing, Inc. p. 308-323

Steinhauer, P. (1997) *Methods of Developing Resiliency in Children from Disadvantaged Populations.* Prepared for the National Forum on Health

Stout, M.D. (1996) *Aboriginal Childhood Agency in the Making.* (Unpublished manuscript), Ottawa: The Centre for Aboriginal Education, Research and Culture, Carleton University

Suomi, S. (1993) "Social and Biological Pathways that Contribute to Variations in Health Status: Evidence from Primate Studies" in *Prosperity, Health and Well-Being.* Proceedings of 11th Honda Foundation Discoveries Symposium. October 16-18, 1993. Toronto. p. 105-112

Suomi, S. (1991) "Early Stress and Adult Emotional Reactivity in Rhesus Monkeys" in *Childhood Environment and Adult Disease.* Wiley, Chichester: Ciba Foundation Symposium 156, p. 171-188

Sylva K. (1994) "School Influences on Children's Development." *Journal of Child Psychology and Psychiatry*, Vol. 35, No. 1, 135-170

Sylva, K. (1992) "Conversations in the Nursery: How They Contribute to Aspirations and Plans." *Language and Education* 6, 141-148

Torjman, S. (1997) *Civic Society: Reclaiming Our Humanity.* Ottawa: The Caledon Institute of Social Policy

Toronto Board of Education (1989) *Scope*, Vol. 4, No. 2

Toronto Board of Education (1991) *Scope*, Vol. 6, No. 2

Tremblay, R. & Craig, W. (1995) "Developmental Crime Prevention" in M. Tonry & D.P. Farrington (eds), *Building a Safer Society: Strategic Approaches to Crime Prevention*. Chicago: University of Chicago Press. p. 151-236

Tremblay, R., Kurtz, L., Masse, L., Vitaro, F., & Pihl, R. (1994) *A Bimodal Preventive Intervention for Disruptive Kindergarten Boys: Its Impact Through Adolescence*. (Unpublished manuscript), Montreal: Research Unit on Children's Psychosocial Maladjustment, University of Montreal

Vanier Institute of the Family (1997) "Canada's Kids: Thriving or Just Surviving?" *Transition* March

Vanier Institute of the Family (1994) *Canadian Families*. Ottawa

Vygotsky, L.S. [1934] (1986) *Thought and Language*, trans. A. Kozulin. Cambridge, Massachusetts: MIT Press

Wadhwani, Z. (1996) *Young Voices*. (Unpublished manuscript)

Werner, E. (1996) Presentation to the Forum of the Centre for Studies of Children at Risk, June 13, 1996. Hamilton, Ontario

Werner, E. & Smith, R. (1992) *Overcoming the Odds: High Risk Children from Birth to Adulthood*. New York: Cornell University Press

White, J. (1997) *Building Caring Communities: Five Capacities That Build Communities and Ten Things Funders Can Do to Support Them*. Presentation to Pragma Council, Spring Conference, April 10, School of Urban and Regional Planning, University of Waterloo

Wilkins, R., Sherman, G. & Best, P. (1991) "Birth Outcomes and Infant Mortality by Income in Urban Canada, 1986." *Health Reports*, Vol. 3, No. 1. Ottawa: Minister of Industry, Science and Technology, Canada

Wilkinson, R. (1994) "The Epidemiological Transition: From Material Scarcity to Social Disadvantage?" Daedalus: Health and Wealth. *Journal of the American Academy of Arts and Sciences*. Fall, 61-77

Willms, J.D. (1997) *Quality and Inequality in Children's Literacy: The Effects of Families, Schools and Communities*. Draft for forthcoming edited volume for the Human Development Program of the Canadian Institute for Advanced Research

Willms, J.D. (1996A) "Indicators of Mathematics Achievement in Canadian Elementary Schools" in *Growing Up in Canada: National Longitudinal Survey of Children and Youth*. Ottawa: Human Resources Development Canada & Statistics Canada. p. 69-82

Willms, J.D. (1996B) *Literacy Skills of Canadian Youth*. Fredericton: Atlantic Centre for Policy Research in Education, University of New Brunswick

Willms, J.D. & Jacobsen, S. (1990) "Growth in Mathematics Skills during the Intermediate Years: Sex Differences and School Effects." *International Journal of Educational Research*, 14, p. 157-174

Zigler, E., & Styfco, S. (eds) (1994) *Headstart and Beyond: A National Plan for Extended Intervention*. New Haven & London: Yale University Press